Date Due

Final Report of the Human Resource Management Project

The Canadian Workplace in Transition

Gordon Betcherman, Kathryn McMullen,
Norm Leckie, and Christina Caron

Industrial Relations Centre
Queen's University at Kingston

ISBN 0-88886-406-X
© 1994, IRC Press
Industrial Relations Centre
Queen's University
Kingston, Ontario
Canada K7L 3N6

Printed and bound in Canada

Publications' Orders: 613 545-6709 or
1-800-361-2456

Canadian Cataloguing in Publication Data

The Canadian workplace in transition
(Human resource management project series)
"Final report of the Human Resource Management Project."
Includes bibliographical references.
ISBN 0-88886-406-X

1. Personnel management – Canada. I. Betcherman, Gordon.
II. Queen's University (Kingston, Ont.).
Industrial Relations Centre. III. Series.

HF5549.2.C3C35 1994   658.3'00971   C94-932016-1

Table of Contents

Foreword

This volume will be of interest to many groups – business executives, union leaders, academics, policy makers, politicians, the media, and others. The reason is obvious. The report is very timely and it addresses issues that reach the public consciousness almost every day. New techniques and innovations to manage the workplace, the use of human resources as a source of competitive advantage, union-management partnership, work and family issues, and technological change are just some of the topics dealt with in the report.

The Canadian economy, like most world economies, is going through very profound changes. These are discussed in the report. They, in turn, have forced management and labour in Canada to respond and adapt. The result is a workplace that does seem to be changing. But what is reality and what is rhetoric.The 'HRM Project' set out to discover the policies and practices actually being utilized at a set of major Canadian organizations to meet the challenges of the 1990s. The research team have succeeded in writing a report which breaks new ground in our understanding of the Canadian workplace and the high performance workplace model of the future. It is the hope of the Industrial Relations Centre that the volume will stimulate further research and analysis of HRM issues.

The Industrial Relations Centre is proud to have been the sponsor of the HRM Project. The Project was a two-year undertaking that consumed the time and effort of many people. It brought together a research team from the former Economic Council of Canada and a network of scholars from Queen's University and across the country. Each of the studies published by IRC Press, including this the final report, were subject to double blind review by two referees. Finally, from start to finish the Project involved the investment of considerable energy and time by the administrative staff of the Industrial Relations Centre.

We are particularly grateful to Industry Canada and Human Resource Development Canada, the primary funders of the Project, for their financial assistance, to Keith Newton who acted as liaison for the federal government, and to the Advisory Committee for their support throughout the Project. I also would like to thank the many scholars who participated in the research project and refereeing process. Special thanks go to Judith Maxwell, former Economic Council of Canada Chair, for serving as Chair of the Project Advisory Committee, to Project Director Gordon Betcherman and to his research team of Kathryn McMullen, Norm Leckie and Christina Caron. My thanks, too, to Carol Williams and her editorial and desktop publishing staff at IRC Press, the publishing arm of the Industrial Relations Centre, for their dedication and skill.

BRYAN M. DOWNIE

Director
Industrial Relations Centre
Queen's University at Kingston

Advisory Committee Members

Judith Maxwell (Chair)
Executive Director
Queen's-University of Ottawa
Economic Projects

Gordon Betcherman
Project Director
Queen's-University of Ottawa
Economic Projects

Bob Baldwin
Research Director
Canadian Labour Force Development Board

Reg Basken
Executive Vice-President
Communications, Energy and Paperworkers Union

Diane Bellemare
Faculty of Administrative Sciences
University of Quebec at Montreal

Jim Cameron
Director, Industrial Relations
General Motors of Canada Limited

Ken Delaney
Research Director
United Steelworkers of America

Tom Kochan
Sloan School of Management
Massachusetts Institute of Technology

Pradeep Kumar
School of Industrial Relations
Queen's University

Harvey Lazar
Senior Assistant Deputy Minister
Human Resource Development Canada

Keith Newton
Special Advisor
Industry Canada

Andrew Sharpe
Research Advisor
Canadian Labour Market and Productivity Centre

Sherran Slack
Vice-President, Human Resources
Warner-Lambert Canada

Anil Verma
Faculty of Management
University of Toronto

Caroline Weber
School of Industrial Relations
Queen's University

1

The Evolution of Human Resource Management in Canada

Opening Up the Black Box

Human resource management is more than just postindustrial-speak. It describes how people are organized in the workplace, and as such shapes the quality of their jobs as well as their economic contribution. Human resource management (HRM) encompasses everything from the employees' strategic role in a long-term business plan, through formal employment practices in areas such as training and compensation, to the day-to-day interaction among workers in the office or on the shop floor.

For much of the past half-century, very little thought was given to HRM practices in Canadian workplaces. By and large, business was good, employment was steady, and the prevailing approaches to industrial relations and personnel administration effectively balanced the interests of employers, employees, and society.

Over the past two decades, however, all of this has changed. First, overall economic performance has deteriorated. Productivity and income growth are down, while unemployment, inequality of earnings, and general economic insecurity are up. Second, the workplace environment has been turned on its head. Business competition has intensified everywhere, creating immense pressure on employers to reduce costs and improve productivity and quality. The revolution in information technology has radically altered the production process, and with it traditional notions of hierarchy, skill, and efficiency. And the labour force itself has changed dramatically with the increasing participation of women, the huge numbers of highly educated baby-boomers, and the ethnic diversity of new entrants.

Workers everywhere now worry about the ability of the system to deliver stable employment, adequate wages and benefits, career-development opportunities, healthy and interesting work, and the support to enable them to deal with family responsibilities. Employers are concerned about their capacity to exploit the promise of the new technologies, about the quality and commitment of their workers, and about the competitiveness of their labour costs. Unions are uncertain about how best to represent today's workers in today's workplaces, while governments search for new policy recipes that will spark human capital investment, innovation, and smooth adjustment to economic change.

The common thread running through all of this uncertainty is that longstanding approaches to human resource management can no longer deliver the goods. In the jargon of the theorists, the shift in the 'technoeconomic paradigm' – from a stable, mass-production, goods economy to a turbulent, flexible-production, information economy – requires a corresponding shift in our social institutions, including the institution of the workplace.

In a future where economic growth will be driven not by natural resources and physical effort but rather by ideas and knowledge, human resource management must change dramatically. How it changes will matter a great deal for business performance, the welfare of workers, and ultimately the health of the economy and society.

Unfortunately, HRM and the organization of Canadian workplaces remain largely a 'black box' to researchers, practitioners, and decision-makers alike. Very little is known about current practices, their impact on business and labour, and the HRM approaches that will be most effective in the future.

Over the past two years, the Human Resource Management Project has peered into this black box in order to better understand the dominant workplace trends in Canada. Specifically, our analysis has focused on the following three questions:

- How are Canadian firms responding to the changing environment in terms of their HRM strategies?

- What are the consequences of these HRM trends for Canadian employers and workers?
- How can business, labour, and government encourage the diffusion of workplace models that promote economic efficiency, security, and equity, while building on Canadian strengths and values?

To address these questions, we have drawn on a range of different methodologies, a variety of new data, and the expertise of specialists from across the country.[1] In this study we present our major findings and discuss their implications for Canadian business, labour, governments, and society.

HRM in Historical Perspective

Two HRM approaches have dominated North American workplaces since World War Two, one that has applied primarily to blue-collar employment and the other to white-collar employment. Osterman (1988) has labelled these the 'industrial' and 'salaried' models, respectively. These employment systems, which evolved gradually through the first half of the century, were sustainable because they incorporated acceptable tradeoffs to accommodate the conflicting interests of workers and employers in security and flexibility, respectively.

The Industrial and Salaried HRM Models

The *industrial* or blue-collar model has typically, though not exclusively, been applied to union settings. It is governed by detailed rules and procedures, many of which are formally negotiated by management and the union and enforced by a grievance-arbitration process. This model is characterized by narrow, rigid job definitions and classifications, seniority-based assignment, no job security (but layoffs according to seniority), and wages attached to jobs.

In the industrial model, the employer's prerogative to manage is broad in many respects. For example, the absence of constraints with regard to job security provides management with an important degree of flexibility in varying the workforce as it sees fit. However, labour is able to regulate important aspects of the workplace through the negotiated system of job classifications and seniority rules. This 'job control unionism' constrains management in how it can reduce the workforce and it protects workers from managerial arbitrariness or favouritism.

The *salaried* model generally has applied to white-collar employees in nonunionized workplaces. This system operates on premises quite different from those describing the industrial model. Jobs tend to be more broadly defined. Decisions about compensation, job assignment, and promotion are based less on seniority than on employers' perceptions of merit. And, unlike the industrial model, there is a general commitment on the part of employers to job security (after a probationary period has been completed).

The tradeoffs in the salaried model are very different from those in the industrial model. In the salaried model management has much more flexibility to organize and assign work, but much less to decide on the overall complement of employees. It provides workers with employment security and greater opportunities to benefit from good performance; however, the price for these is the expectation that they will be committed to the organization and they will have no protection from managerial subjectivity.

The Success of the Traditional Models

These HRM systems served us well for the first three decades after World War Two. Productivity growth was strong, wages increased in tandem, and unemployment rates were very low. While this robust economic performance obviously cannot be attributed exclusively to HRM practices, it suggests that the organization of Canadian workplaces was compatible with strong growth and a relatively equitable distribution of the benefits of that growth.

The features of the traditional HRM models 'fit' well with the environment in which they were designed to operate. They provided an employment system that offered stability and certainty through clearly defined rules and procedures. And stability and certainty were what was required in an environment where growth was virtually assured if the powerful economic machine could be kept running.

Indeed, the environment in which North American workplaces operated in the first three decades after the war was favourable and relatively straightforward. Markets were expanding and there was little foreign competition. While technological change did occur, it essentially involved incremental improvements in the technology of mass production that allowed firms to increasingly exploit economies of scale. The labour force was homogeneous and dominated by prime-aged male workers, and legal and regulatory requirements were uncomplicated. During the past two decades, however, all of these conditions have changed dramatically.

Growing Pressure on the Traditional Models

Pressure on the traditional HRM systems started building in the 1970s. This was most evident in the US, where unions, and by extension the industrial model, came under increasing attack from employers. In Canada, the challenge has been characteristically somewhat delayed and more moderate. Certainly, the fact that the labour movement in this country has been stronger and more assertive is an important reason for this difference.

Nevertheless, in the final analysis, the traditional approaches have been challenged here and in the US for the same reasons: first, deteriorating economic outcomes, and second, serious doubts that the old models can deliver the goods in an environment of fierce global competition and rapid technological change.

Deteriorating Outcomes

A number of trends indicate that there was an economic u-turn in the mid-1970s. Productivity growth slowed down considerably in the second half of that decade and even more in the 1980s (Figure 1). This slowdown, and the attendant decline in competitiveness, caused concern about industrial efficiency and performance.

Inevitably, the weak economic trend had negative consequences for labour as the productivity slowdown translated into stagnant wage growth (Figure 2). The unemployment rate rose in the 1970s and has continued to ratchet upwards since then. And the distribution of earnings has become more unequal and more polarized (Morissette, Myles, and Picot 1993).

The New Environment and the Old Models

Although the long-term economic problems affect everybody, pressure for change in the workplace has originated with management. Two factors were particularly important – growing and increasingly global competition and the microelectronic revolution that has radically altered the technology of production.

Figure 1

The Productivity Slowdown: Change in Real Output per Person-Hour,
10-Year Averages, Canada, 1950s to 1990-92

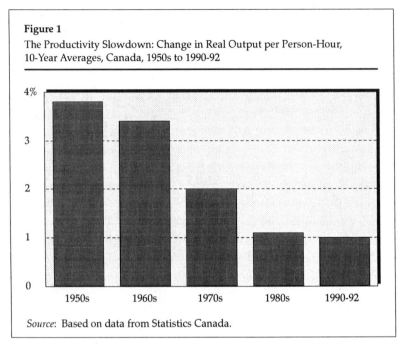

Source: Based on data from Statistics Canada.

Figure 2

Hourly Wages and Salaries, Canada, 1967-91

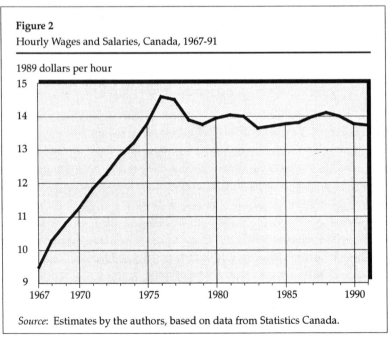

Source: Estimates by the authors, based on data from Statistics Canada.

Competition presented the challenge; the new technologies and cost containment were seen as the solution. However, in the 1980s, as firms started to pursue cost and innovation driven competitive advantage, many began to see the industrial model as part of the problem. Narrow job classifications, seniority-based deployment rules, the lack of individual incentives, and the lack of labour input into decision-making were increasingly perceived as constraints on flexibility and the causes of rigid cost structures. If lean production and flexible specialization were going to work in Canada, the traditional industrial model needed to change.[2]

The efficacy of the salaried model has really only come under scrutiny during the 1990s. In many respects, it has the features necessary for the new economy – broad job classifications, merit-based deployment, and rewards linked to performance. What has become an issue for employers is the job security pledge and the constraint this places on their ability to control labour costs. As payrolls become increasingly dominated by white-collar employment and the labour-saving potential of office technologies expands, pressure on the traditional salaried model grows.

While the traditional models were challenged by employers initially, recently some unions have also taken up the issue of workplace reorganization. Labour's response is in part a recognition that HRM reform is irreversibly on the business agenda, and in part an acknowledgement that the old models, at least as they now function, are not serving workers well either.

A New Human Resource Management Model?

With the traditional HRM approaches in flux, the question now is, what is the appropriate model for a high-technology, competitive environment? In very stylized terms, two paths are possible.

The Low Labour-Cost Path

On this path businesses compete by cutting costs. This strategy has characterized the response of certain parts of US industry. Research suggests it has not been quite as prevalent here, presumably because Canadian unions are stronger (Chaykowski and Verma 1992).

Nevertheless, the numbers of layoffs in recent years, the slow rebound in hiring after the recession, and the growth of part-time and other nonstandard jobs all point to the fact that containing labour costs is an important strategy here as well. Immediate economic pressures ensure that firms must be conscious of how their cost structures compare with those of other producers, both domestic and foreign. Certainly, with the integration of the North American economies, comparisons between Canadian and US costs have become more germane. Canadian firms, in fact, have lost the labour-cost advantage they had over their American counterparts during the 1980s, at least in manufacturing (Table 1).

Ultimately, the limitations of a Canadian HRM model that is based on low labour costs must be acknowledged. The sheer magnitude of the labour-cost gap between Canada and many countries, particularly the newly industrialized countries, makes it unlikely that we could ever compete successfully purely on a cost basis (Table 1).

The High-Performance Path

This path involves directing workplace reform towards a 'high-performance' model. The underlying rationale is the proposition that a high-wage country like Canada can only compete and maintain its standard of living through what Porter (1990) has called a

Table 1

Index Comparing Hourly Compensation Costs[1] for Manufacturing Production Workers, Canada and Selected Countries and Regions, Selected Years, 1975 – 1991

Country	1975	1980	1985	1988	1991
Canada	100	100	100	100	100
United States	110	118	120	103	89
European Community[2]	87	118	73	105	102
Germany	110	147	89	135	128
France	78	107	70	96	88
United Kingdom	57	89	57	77	78
Japan	53	67	60	95	83
Asian NICs[2]	9	14	15	19	24
Mexico	na	na	15	10	13

Source: Based on data from the US Bureau of Labor Statistics.

na = not available.
[1] Compensation costs include pay for time worked, other direct pay, and employers' expenditures on public and private benefit plans.
[2] Trade-weighted average. The Asian NICs are Hong Kong, Korea, Singapore, and Taiwan.

'differentiation' strategy – winning markets through product innovation, quality, service, and specialization.

A 'high-performance' model can take many possible forms. It builds on the argument that in an environment characterized by a high degree of competitiveness and flexible technologies, production must emphasize quality and innovation.[3] The kind of workforce that can meet these market demands must be highly skilled, committed, and flexible. An HRM approach that would support a workforce of this quality is likely to include the following elements:

- a flexible work organization;
- a commitment to training;
- employee involvement and participation in decision-making;
- policies to promote the sharing of benefits and risks.

On paper the high-performance path is now widely accepted as the direction in which workplace reform must go. Indeed, its broad outline has been endorsed in recent policy statements from several unions, the business community, and federal and provincial governments. Nonetheless, groups such as these may have fundamentally different ideas about what constitutes a high-performance workplace specifically. Certainly, there are differences of opinion regarding the roles, responsibilities, and entitlements of each of the actors. These differences, and how they play out, will shape the future face of HRM systems in this country.

The Research Framework

The broad framework underlying our analysis is set out in Figure 3.[4] We have followed the structure of this framework in reporting our research.

In Chapter 2, we examine the two key sets of factors that shape HRM systems at the level of the firm: the environment and the strategic choices made by the actors. A major theme of our research is that the environment has fundamentally changed in many ways, and that these changes have placed substantial pressure on the traditional approaches to HRM. However, as we shall see, HRM practices are not mechanically dictated by environmental conditions: employers, workers, unions, governments, and other institutions also play a role through the strategies they adopt and the choices they make.

Figure 3
The Conceptual Framework for the Human Resource Management Project

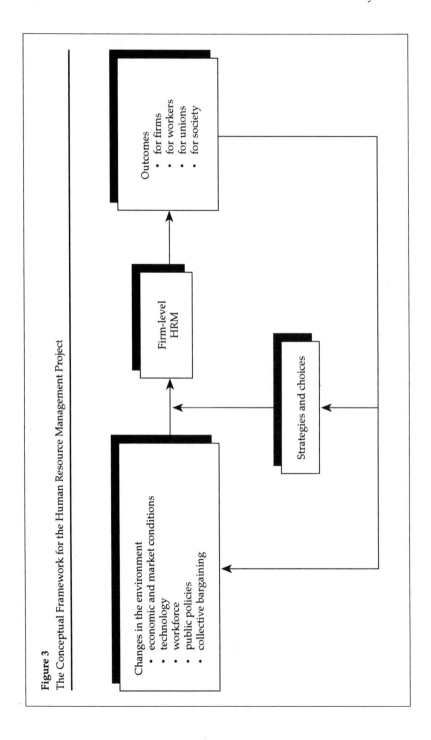

We turn to the HRM practices of Canadian firms in Chapter 3. 'Human resource management' refers to the gamut of firm-level strategies, policies, and activities relating to the organization of people in the workplace. Our evidence on HRM trends covers a wide range of functional areas including job design, selection and staffing, training and development, communications, employee involvement, scheduling, compensation, and union-management relations. We suggest that these functional areas should not be viewed in isolation but instead as interdependent parts of a firm-level HRM system. Using new survey data, we find that three distinct HRM-system patterns can be identified among Canadian establishments.

Human resource management practices have important social, political, and economic implications for employers, employees, and unions as well as for the economy and society. In Chapter 4, we report on our results linking HRM approach and firm performance. In Chapter 5, we turn to the implications of HRM trends for Canadian workers and their unions. Finally, in Chapter 6, we present the conclusions and implications of our research. We begin with a summary of what we have learned from our empirical investigation. We then sketch out the main ingredients of a Canadian HRM model for the new economy. Finally, we put forward some suggestions about how the principles of this model can be widely diffused.

Notes

[1] The individual studies that were undertaken as part of the Human Resource Management Project are listed in Appendix A. In particular, we relied on three new survey databases developed for this project. For background information on these surveys, including technical details, see Appendix B.

[2] According to Kochan, Katz, and McKersie (1986), an important part of this story as it unfolded in the US was the pent up anti-union animus within the employer community. In Canada, according to existing evidence, this appears to have been less of a factor.

[3] This discussion is based on Verma and Weiler (1994).

[4] This framework is representative of the dominant approach in current industrial relations and human resource management research. It is based on the traditional systems model associated with Dunlop (1958) and augmented by the strategic-choice model developed by Kochan, Katz, and McKersie (1986).

2

Environmental Pressures and Strategic Responses

In this chapter, we examine two sets of factors that shape HRM systems: the environment and the strategic choices of business and labour. Beginning with the environment, we draw on our survey data and national statistics to summarize the main elements of the new landscape – greater competition, rapid technological innovation, a changing workforce, and an increasing number of regulatory requirements.

We then consider the strategic choices Canadian business and labour are making in response to the pressures created by the new environment. We look first at employers; our focus is on overall business strategy because choices made at this level delineate what is possible in the workplace. We then examine the choices that Canadian unions are facing, in particular their responses to the competitive initiatives of business.

The Changing Environment

In the analysis for this chapter, we have relied extensively on the Human Resource Practices Survey (HRPS), which was carried out in 1993 for the HRM Project. This survey gathered detailed information from 714 establishments across Canada on their HRM practices and policies. The sample was drawn from four sectors selected to reflect the broad range of industries in the Canadian economy: a resource group (wood products), a high-value-added manufacturing industry (electrical and electronic products), a more traditional manufacturing industry (fabricated metal products), and a dynamic service group (selected business services).[1]

More Competitive Markets

The HRPS asked respondents about important changes that had taken place in their organizational environment over the previous five years, since 1988 (Table 2). The change most often cited was an increase in the degree of competition. This is consistent with the results of interviews with human resource executives conducted by Downie and Coates (1994) for the HRM Project. These executives, representing 16 major corporations in a variety of industries, identified growing competition, both domestic and international, as the single major pressure on their organizations.

Indeed, our survey data also indicate that more competitive markets have become a universal fact of life for Canadian industry. It is unusual to find enterprises that are not facing more intense competition now than they were 5 or 10 years ago. And while much of that

Table 2

Proportion of Establishments Reporting Significant Changes in the External Business Environment, by Sector, 1988-93

Change	Wood products	Fabricated metal products	Electrical and electronic products	Selected business services	All sectors
			(Percent)		
Increase in the degree of competition	69.2	84.0	84.4	78.7	78.9
Regulatory requirements	74.4	71.3	66.4	67.8	70.2
Technology	63.3	56.9	72.7	71.1	65.7
Foreign-market orientation	53.3	43.4	59.5	50.3	51.2
Senior management	44.5	49.1	60.0	48.2	49.9
Product or service	34.2	36.8	51.9	43.8	41.2
Controlling ownership	42.6	30.1	42.7	28.8	35.5

Source: Estimates by the authors, based on data from the Human Resource Practices Survey.

competition is North American in origin, the share originating elsewhere is also becoming significant (Figure 4).

Very fundamental changes have taken place in the nature of competition as well. There is less emphasis on high-volume, standardized output and more on specialized, 'niche' products and services. This has made knowledge, skills, and creativity increasingly important for Canadian businesses. Not surprisingly, then, the search is on for ways of organizing work and managing people that tap these factors.

Technological Change

Since the 1970s, technological systems have been transformed by computers and innovations in communications that have affected all industries and virtually all activities within firms. This has had important organizational implications, because efficient production requires a good 'fit' between technology and organization. As a result, organizational designs developed for mass-production technologies must be refitted in order for the new technologies to be used most effectively. A consensus has emerged that the necessary changes include flatter hierarchies, decentralized decision-making, and flexible operational procedures.

We have drawn on data from the Working With Technology Survey (WWTS) to examine the spread and impact of computer-based technologies (CBT) in Canadian industry. The WWTS sample consists of 224 establishments from across Canada and from all sectors except agriculture, construction, and government. The unique feature of these data is their longitudinal nature: respondents were surveyed in 1985 and then again in 1991 about their experiences with CBT over the preceding five years (1980-85 and 1986-91).[2]

The WWTS panel data show dramatic increases in the introduction of CBT over the two survey periods. For example, the proportion of employees working directly with the technologies increased from 15.3 percent in 1985 to 37 percent in 1991. The longer and more continuous experience of those adopting CBT early is reflected in the particularly high share of their employees who worked directly with CBT by 1991 (Figure 5). These data suggest that the diffusion pattern has two dimensions: the spread has become more *extensive* as former nonusers have introduced the technologies; and it has become more *intensive* as earlier users have put more CBT into place, deepening its penetration within their operations.

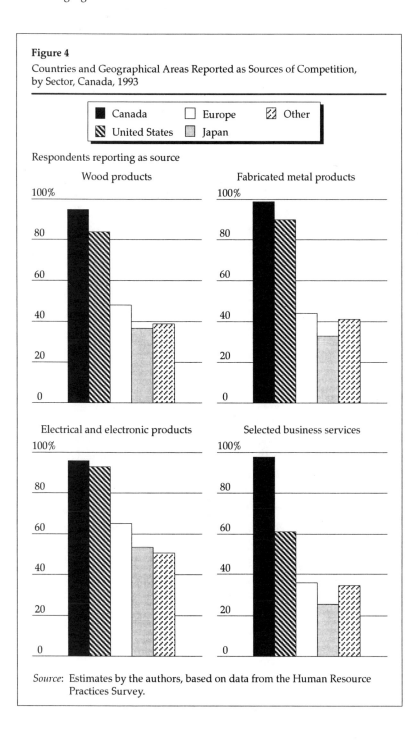

Figure 4

Countries and Geographical Areas Reported as Sources of Competition, by Sector, Canada, 1993

■ Canada □ Europe ▧ Other
▨ United States ▦ Japan

Respondents reporting as source

Wood products

Fabricated metal products

Electrical and electronic products

Selected business services

Source: Estimates by the authors, based on data from the Human Resource Practices Survey.

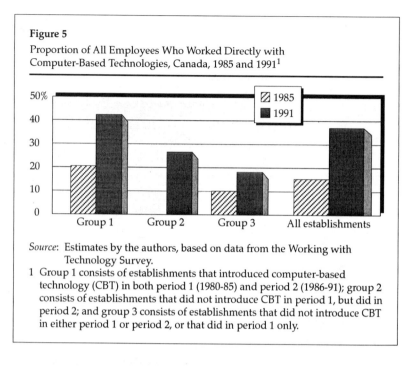

Figure 5

Proportion of All Employees Who Worked Directly with
Computer-Based Technologies, Canada, 1985 and 1991[1]

Source: Estimates by the authors, based on data from the Working with
Technology Survey.

1 Group 1 consists of establishments that introduced computer-based
technology (CBT) in both period 1 (1980-85) and period 2 (1986-91); group 2
consists of establishments that did not introduce CBT in period 1, but did in
period 2; and group 3 consists of establishments that did not introduce CBT
in either period 1 or period 2, or that did in period 1 only.

Computer-based technologies also grew in sophistication over the
survey period. There was a shift away from stand-alone applications,
such as word processors and work stations, to more integrated
data/communications networks. With this, the organizational impact
of the technologies has become much more far-reaching.[3]

The Impacts of CBT on Workers' Skills[4]

A critical human-resource issue associated with the diffusion of CBT
concerns their impact on workers' skills. The conventional view is that
technological change upskills work by eliminating the most routine
tasks and creating demand for more technical sophistication. In contrast, the 'deskilling' hypothesis argues that new technologies tend to
supplant workers' skills, automating many 'craft-like' jobs and cur-
tailing opportunities for workers' creativity and ingenuity. A third
view is that the impact is not predetermined, but instead depends on
the choices employers make in deciding how they will use the technologies.

To consider this issue, the WWTS analysis organized the establishments surveyed into three equal-sized groups – 'high-tech,' 'mid-

tech,' and 'low-tech' – ranked according to the proportion of the workforce using CBT in 1991. The skill levels of employees were then compared across these groups (Figure 6).[5] The establishments reporting the most extensive use of CBT had far more high-skilled and far less low-skilled employees than the other establishments. Multiple regression analysis confirmed this finding. The results of this analysis are summarized in Appendix C1.

As computerization proceeds, then, firms must develop the capacity to meet the increased skill requirements. This will be critical if the potential of the new technologies for enhanced productivity, quality, and flexibility is to be achieved.

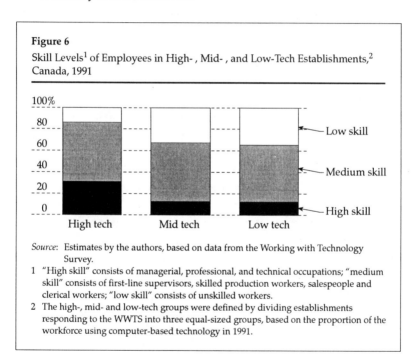

Figure 6

Skill Levels[1] of Employees in High- , Mid- , and Low-Tech Establishments,[2] Canada, 1991

Source: Estimates by the authors, based on data from the Working with Technology Survey.

1 "High skill" consists of managerial, professional, and technical occupations; "medium skill" consists of first-line supervisors, skilled production workers, salespeople and clerical workers; "low skill" consists of unskilled workers.

2 The high-, mid- and low-tech groups were defined by dividing establishments responding to the WWTS into three equal-sized groups, based on the proportion of the workforce using computer-based technology in 1991.

A Workforce in Flux

The Canadian labour force is now older, more highly educated, more ethnically diverse, and includes a much higher proportion of women than it did 20 years ago. These changes are exerting pressure on employers to respond to employees who have new and very different characteristics and expectations.

More Educated and Older Workers

Over time, the average educational attainment of successive groups of young labour-market entrants has risen. As a result of this process and the retirement of older workers (typically with fewer years of schooling), an increasing proportion of the labour force has secondary and postsecondary schooling.

At the same time, however, changing demographic trends mean that the share of young workers in the labour force has been falling and will continue to fall through this decade. This will limit the contribution that young, highly educated new entrants can make to labour-force renewal. The great majority of workers who will be in the labour force 10 to 20 years from now are already there. Consequently, in order to get the skills they need, employers will have to rely more on retraining than they did in the past when new supplies of educated workers were plentiful.

Growth in the Labour Force Participation of Women

Over the past two decades, the proportion of women in the labour force has increased from 34 to 45 percent. There has been, in particular, a dramatic increase in the participation of prime-aged women, including those with school-aged children. This increase in the number of female workers is placing various pressures on traditional approaches to human resource management.

One important source of pressure relates to the need for workers to balance their work and family responsibilities. For many women (and to a far lesser degree, some men), this balance is very difficult to achieve without more flexible employment arrangements. One result has been the dramatic growth in part-time work from 10.6 percent of total employment in 1975 to 16.8 percent in 1992.[6] Research indicates that the preference among women for part-time work is closely linked to their family responsibilities. Indeed, a recent survey undertaken by Duxbury and Higgins (1994) has found that the overwhelming majority of women working part time had child care or elder care responsibilities.

Important issues have emerged with respect to the growth of part-time employment and nonstandard work more generally. On the one hand, this type of employment is seen by many families as a way of balancing the often conflicting and highly stressful demands arising from work and family responsibilities. On the other hand, however, serious concerns are being raised about the adequacy of earnings, accessibility of nonwage benefits, job security, and opportunities for training and career advancement for nonstandard employees. As a result, employers are under increasing pressure to accommodate flexible schedules, to improve conditions of work for their nonstandard workers, and to provide a range of family-care benefits.

The Increase in Regulatory Requirements

The increasing complexity of the regulatory framework has been another important development. Among HRPS respondents, 70 percent cited changing regulatory requirements as a major factor altering their external business environment. In the human- resource area, regulations concerning employment standards, human rights, employment and pay equity, occupational health and safety, collective bargaining, workers' compensation, unemployment insurance, and pensions all must be taken into account.

The pressure for new labour market regulation has come from two sources.[7] First, domestic and global economic restructuring has created a range of new concerns for workers. These include structural unemployment and wage losses arising from displacement in the labour market, the polarization of earnings, and an increase in the use of part-time and short-term employees. Since the main instrument for adjustment in North America has been the 'external' labour market, the demand for new policy measures to regulate the adjustment process has grown. As a result, we have seen new or expanded regulations regarding advance notice of layoffs, hours and benefits, unemployment insurance, and minimum wage laws, for example.

The second source of pressure for new regulations has come from shifts in the composition of the labour force. The greater participation of women, growing ethnic diversity, and recognition of the special needs of the disabled have led to pay- and employment-equity legislation. And the aging of the workforce has created pressure for new regulations respecting pensions and retirement policies.

The Strategic Responses of Business

The environmental changes, particularly heightened competition, have forced Canadian businesses to rethink how they position themselves in the marketplace. They can consider several options in fashioning their overall business strategies. One is to compete on the basis of cost minimization. Another is to compete through 'differentiation' based on product innovation and high productivity, quality, and service. Or, they can pick a position in between.

These options will ultimately influence the HRM approach taken by the firm. For example, a strategy based on competing through low costs involves few incentives to develop what we have called a 'high-performance' workplace. Instead, it more likely calls for operating strategies designed to exploit economies of scale, Taylorist forms of work organization, and human-resource practices that minimize investment in the workforce. Differentiation, on the other hand, involves quite different incentives. Competing through innovation and quality creates the need for the commitment to training, sharing, and participation that define the high-performance workplace model.[8]

Current Strategies Among Canadian Firms

Establishments responding to the Human Resource Practices Survey were asked to identify the ingredients in their current business strategy. The results indicate that their strategies tend to include a number of elements. Most commonly cited were reducing operating (nonlabour) costs, increasing employees' skills, developing new products/markets, reducing labour costs, and introducing new technology. Least often cited were undertaking R&D and enhancing labour-management cooperation (Figure 7).

Further analysis of the data reveals patterns in these elements. For example, firms that cited reducing labour costs were also likely to cite reducing other costs ($r=.50$). Similarly, increasing employees' skills and enhancing labour-management cooperation were significantly correlated ($r=.32$), as were introducing new technology and developing new products/markets ($r=.22$).

It is interesting to note that the first of these correlations describes a cost-based strategic orientation, while the second and third are consistent with HR-based and innovation-based orientations, respectively. How frequently were each of these pairs of elements jointly reported? The cost-based pair was most common, cited by 60.9 percent of the sample. The innovation-based pair followed, reported by 50.6 percent of the respondents. Notably, the HR-based strategy was least common (44.4 percent) among establishments surveyed.

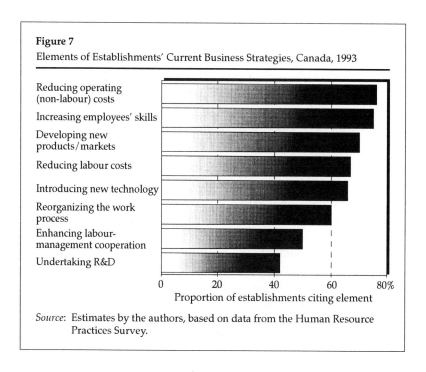

Figure 7
Elements of Establishments' Current Business Strategies, Canada, 1993

Reducing operating (non-labour) costs

Increasing employees' skills

Developing new products/markets

Reducing labour costs

Introducing new technology

Reorganizing the work process

Enhancing labour-management cooperation

Undertaking R&D

0   20   40   60   80%
Proportion of establishments citing element

Source: Estimates by the authors, based on data from the Human Resource Practices Survey.

In order to examine business strategy patterns more systematically, factor analysis was applied to the survey data on the eight strategic elements identified in Figure 7. Three factors emerged clearly:

- The first, which we have called *process*, captures the four strategic elements concerned with improving the operational process within the firm: increasing employees' skills, introducing new technology, reorganizing the work process, and enhancing labour-management cooperation.
- The second, *cost*, is primarily a combination of the two cost-reduction strategies: reducing labour and operating (nonlabour) costs.
- The third, *product*, essentially loads on two strategic elements concerned with gaining market position through product innovation: undertaking R&D and developing new products/markets.[9]

The survey data indicate that the importance of the strategic factors varies by establishment characteristics such as sector, size, and union status.[10] Business strategies that involve the process factor – those that tap human resources, new technology, and work reorganization – were most prevalent in the electrical and electronic products industry, in large establishments, and where a union was present.

Executive Interviews

Qualitative evidence on the strategic choices of Canadian firms comes from the interviews with human-resource executives (Downie and Coates 1994). These findings are consistent with the HRPS results.[11] The elements of these organizations' business strategies appear to incorporate differentiation or cost-cutting, and in some cases a combination of the two (Table 3). Technological change and improvements in quality are part of virtually all the corporations' competitive strategies. At least one-half also cited productivity/efficiency gains and various cost-cutting measures, including the sale of assets, closures and rationalization, and reducing labour costs as important elements in their current business strategy.

Downie and Coates found that human resource management is taking on somewhat more strategic importance. For example, several firms were increasing communications with employees, sharing information, and making greater investments in training. This process tended to be more developed in nonunionized organizations than in unionized ones. While improved labour relations were reported in some unionized establishments, the traditional adversarial relation-

Table 3

Strategic Responses to Economic Pressures by 16 Corporations[1], Canada, 1992

Response	Number of corporations
Technological change	14
Quality improvements	14
Productivity/efficiency gains	11
Sale of assets	10
Closures, rationalization	10
Reducing labour costs	8
Mergers and acquisitions	7
Process improvements	6

Source: Based on Downie and Coates (1994), Table 3.

[1] Corporations might include several of these elements in their response.

ship largely remains. Very few of the corporations interviewed were really trying to bring the union into a genuine workplace partnership.

While many business strategies have incorporated improved quality and innovation, the most typical strategic responses to the increasingly competitive environment were downsizing and introducing new technology. In most firms, the layoffs, cost-cutting, and uncertainty that have resulted from the dominant competitive strategies have overwhelmed the positive impact that might have been achieved through new HRM initiatives. This has made it difficult to create and sustain positive, innovative workplace strategies.

Union Strategies

As employers have pursued lean production and other workplace reorganization strategies, unions have faced an apparent dilemma. One option was to resist the management initiatives, be viewed as out-of-touch special interest groups, and risk losing bargaining units and jobs as employers sought out nonunionized locations. The second was to passively cooperate, be seen as captive to management's agenda, and risk accepting a restructuring process that might not be in the interests of workers. There is also a third option that is being considered by some Canadian unions: to develop a strategy for workplace restructuring that integrates labour's objectives with management's competitiveness imperative.

The State of Canadian Unions

The choice a union makes among these options will be determined by a number of factors, including its vibrancy and relative strength. For example, in the US, where organized labour has been in steady decline since the 1970s, unions have often had little choice but to accept management's restructuring initiatives.

Certainly, unions are experiencing difficult times here as well; their bargaining strength has decreased and union density has been declining in the private sector.[12] Nevertheless, organized labour is clearly in a stronger position in Canada than in the US. The most obvious indicator is overall membership: trends in the two countries began diverging in the 1960s, and by 1992 the Canadian unionization rate was more than double that in the US (Figure 8).

Most observers agree that unions in Canada have much more scope than their US counterparts in responding to management reorganiza-

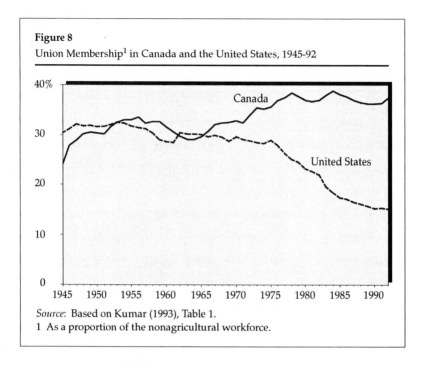

Figure 8
Union Membership[1] in Canada and the United States, 1945-92

Source: Based on Kumar (1993), Table 1.
1 As a proportion of the nonagricultural workforce.

tion strategies. In the face of a stronger labour movement, Canadian employers in many sectors simply cannot impose their competitive strategies to the degree possible in the US.

The Evolution of Labour's Strategic Responses[13]

In certain ways, the 'new' human resource management is inherently problematic for organized labour: it is efficiency-driven and aims to strengthen the direct links between individual workers and the enterprise. Union interests, on the other hand, are traditionally equity-driven and based on collective labour values and representation. Moreover, unions typically have not had ready access to the resources and expertise necessary to develop their own workplace agendas. As a result, they have often resisted management's HRM initiatives.

However, neither simple opposition nor passive cooperation have proven to be effective. Management is generally prepared to act unilaterally in implementing workplace reforms, and if the union is not actively involved there is no mechanism for ensuring that labour's interests, such as improving the quality of the work environment and increasing workplace democracy, will be considered. As a result, labour's strategic responses have recently become more complex and proactive. This is particularly true of some of the larger unions that have the resources to develop a positive agenda for workplace reform.

In his study for the HRM Project, Kumar (1994) examines the positions of the Canadian Auto Workers (CAW), the United Steelworkers (USWA), and the Communications Workers (now part of the Communications, Energy, and Paperworkers and called CWC/CEP). These unions have used their experience over the past decade to move incrementally from resistance to more active intervention in workplace restructuring. While there are differences in the three unions' precise goals, approaches, and strategies, many essential elements of their strategies are ultimately very similar. These include:

- Recognition that workplace restructuring is a global phenomenon and that it will be introduced unilaterally if unions do not get involved;
- Recognition that union involvement is necessary for achieving positive outcomes for workers;
- An adversarial labour-management model characterized by different interests and unequal power;
- Insistence on negotiated workplace change, which extends the traditional boundaries of collective bargaining to include production efficiency;
- A recognition of the value of productivity but an emphasis on the need for a meaningful labour voice in improving it and labour getting a share of the dividend;
- A definition of work reorganization that goes beyond teamwork, employee involvement, and job enlargement to include 'good' job designs (i.e., ones that are safe, healthy, and skill-deepening) and extensive training and retraining opportunities;
- Equal partnership in the conception, development, and implementation of work reorganization; and
- A view of workplace reorganization as part of a broader commitment to industrial and social democracy.

The CAW, USWA, and CWC/CEP agendas clearly show that at least part of the labour movement has moved quite far along in developing a strategic response to the changing environment. However, three cautionary points need to be made about union strategy and its impact on workplace trends. First, the particular agendas studied by Kumar represent the leading edge in thinking within the labour movement. Many unions have not yet formulated such developed strategies. Second, even where the national union has articulated an active strategy, labour's actual response at the workplace level may be quite different. Finally, the real viability of union workplace agendas presumes a willingness on the part of employers to relinquish unilateral control over the design of the work process and the structure of the organization. However, our research, including the executive interviews noted earlier, suggests that this is far from typical.

A study undertaken by Wagar (1994) for the HRM Project reveals that unions rarely take part in strategic decision-making. Among the 367 unionized organizations he surveyed, less than 10 percent indicated that their union was involved in strategic management decision-making. A similar conclusion comes from the Working With Technology Survey: only a minority of the unionized respondents reported that labour was involved in planning for technological change.

Summary

The environment in which Canadian business operates has undergone massive change in the last couple of decades. More intense competition, a technological revolution, changes in the workforce, and an increasingly complex regulatory framework have all contributed to a broad restructuring of the economy and of individual firms. Organizations are being forced to reexamine virtually all of their business practices, beginning with the fundamental question of how they position themselves competitively in the marketplace.

The choices regarding overall business strategy inevitably have important effects on human resource management. Our research indicates that the most common competitive strategies are based on two elements: cutting costs and introducing new technology. Strategies that also explicitly build on the contribution of human resources – through, for example, investment in employees' skills, and increasing workers' involvement in decision-making and labour-management cooperation – are less typical.

Notes

[1] Some technical details on the Human Resource Practices Survey are included in Appendix B. The descriptive results have been published in four sector reports. See Betcherman and Mac Donald (1993a,b) and McMullen and Mac Donald (1993a,b).

[2] Technical details on the Working With Technology Survey are provided in Appendix B. The descriptive results are reported in McMullen, Leckie, and Caron (1993).

[3] For more details on patterns of CBT diffusion, see Betcherman, McMullen, and Leckie (1994).

[4] This discussion is based on a study done by Caron (1993) for the HRM Project.

[5] 'Low-skilled' jobs were those described by employers as unskilled; 'medium-skilled' jobs included sales, clerical, skilled production, and first-line supervisory work; and 'high-skilled' jobs were defined as management, professional, and technical work.

[6] This increase is partly due to a growing number of 'involuntary' part-time workers, that is, workers who would perfer to be employed full-time. The subject of involuntary part-time employment is taken up in Chapter 5.

[7] For more detail, see Gunderson (1993).

[8] These relationships between overall business strategy and HRM approach have received empirical support from other researchers. For example, see Arthur's (1992) analysis based on data collected from US steel minimills.

[9] Factor analysis uses the correlation coefficients among a set of variables to construct a small number of factors that summarize the original data. The factor analysis of the eight busienss strategy elements in the HRPS database indicates that these three factors account for 60 percent of the variation in those elements.

[10] The mean factor scores by various establishment characteristics are presented in Appendix C2.

[11] These corporations were not intended to be representative of Canadian industry. They clearly are in different market situations and many undoubtedly have capabilities and values that are not characteristic of smaller firms. But the environmental pressures they are experiencing are similar to those reported by all companies, with heightened competition heading the list. As well, it is likely that the firms interviewed set many of the standards for their industries in terms of business strategy.

[12] For example, in mining, manufacturing, and construction, which are traditionally unionized, density rates declined by between 10 and 15 percent between 1978 and 1989 (Kumar 1993). And in the private-sector service industries that account for most employment growth now, unions have never established a foothold. One view, albeit a controversial one, is that the state of unionization in the Canadian private sector is essentially following US

trends with a time lag, and that the two will eventually converge (Troy 1992). Other research casts serious doubts on this 'convergence' thesis (for example, Riddell 1992).

[13] This discussion relies heavily on Kumar (1994).

3

Human Resource Management Practices

Although there is a sense that HRM practices are in a state of flux, little serious evidence exists on what is actually happening in the Canadian workplace. To what extent are organizations moving away from traditional HRM models? How prevalent are the 'high-performance workplace' practices?

Relying on our survey databases, we begin by describing prevailing practices in a range of human-resource areas: planning and the HR function, job design, training, compensation, employee participation, flexible scheduling and family-care policies, and the use of part-time and other nonstandard employment.[1]

We then turn to the HRM *systems* – or the complete set of practices – within firms. Our analysis of the Human Resource Practices Survey (HRPS) reveals three distinct models. One includes establishments that follow a 'traditional' system, and two have elements of a high-performance-workplace model – one a 'compensation-based' approach and the other a 'participation-based' approach.

The HR Function

During the past two decades, new demands have been placed on the role, structure, and contribution of the HR function. Downie and Coates (1994), in their executive interviews, identified the emerging model of the HR function as being quite different from the traditional one (Figure 9). The new model is less centralized and bureaucratic and more integrated with overall business strategy and operations. The HR function is being pushed down to the line operations, and the HR department no longer administers services but acts as advisor and consultant to supervisors and teams.

While this model describes how large corporations, at least, are trying to restructure the HR function, Downie and Coates find that the transition has not always been easy. Pushing HR decision-making down to the line has met with resistance from line managers. As well, the participation of human resource managers in strategic decision-making is still very limited; as one HR executive put it, 'the sad reality is that we are still the forgotten sister of the financing and marketing functions' (Downie and Coates 1994). But perhaps the most important brake on moving the HR function forward has been the fact that the attempt to develop a more strategic orientation has occurred at a time when economic pressure is leading to staff cutbacks and hence to low morale.

The HRPS data support the view that human resource managers are often outside the decision-making circle, even when it comes to HR

Figure 9

The Human-Resource Function:
The Traditional and Emerging Models

Traditional Model	Emerging Model
• bureaucratic	• small corporate staff
• centralized	• decentralized to serve and empower the line[1]
• insular	• more integration of line interests
• specialized staff function	• broader range of expertise with more advising, enabling, coaching role
• separate personnel and labour-relations functions	• somewhat more integration between industrial relations and HR

Source: Downie and Coates (1994), Figure 7.
1 Centralized where necessary for consistency and continuity.

issues. To get a sense of decision-making patterns, survey respondents were asked who would make the ultimate decision for their organization in four different (hypothetical) situations, one involving capital-equipment investments and three involving human resources.[2] The results show that, as expected, capital-investment decisions are made exclusively by management, either at the establishment or the headquarters level (Table 4). What is more surprising is how infrequently the HR unit is the decision-maker when it comes to introducing a new training program, self-supervised work teams, or a new wage scheme.[3]

Table 4

Patterns of Decision Making among Canadian Establishments, 1993

	Types of decisions			
Decision maker	Capital investments	Training program	Work teams	Wage scheme
	(Percent)			
Establishment management	68.0	79.2	89.4	69.9
Human resource unit	0.7	12.6	3.9	5.8
Employees or union	0.0	0.4	2.1	2.1
Head office[1]	31.3	7.8	4.5	22.2
Total	100.0	100.0	100.0	100.0

Source: Estimates by the authors, based on data from the Human Resource Practices Survey.
[1] Where applicable.

Formal HR Planning

The extent of formal HR planning and evaluation is an indicator of the sophistication of the HR function in an organization. In all functional areas except compensation, only a minority of HRPS respondents reported having a formal plan (Table 5). Formal evaluation procedures were even less common. Planning and evaluation activities did increase with establishment size; among establishments with over 250 employees, 91.6 percent reported having a formal plan in at least one of the functional areas listed in Table 5, compared with only 60.8 percent among those with less than 50 employees.

Ultimately, the most revealing measure of the strategic role played by the HR function is whether human-resource planning and evaluation are integrated into overall business planning. This was the case

Table 5

Proportion of Establishments with Formal Planning and Evaluation in Human-Resource Functional Areas, 1993

Functional area	Formal plan	Formal evaluation procedures
	(Percent)	
Job design/analysis	39.4	33.4
Staffing	38.4	27.3
Training/development	44.7	30.6
Compensation	58.2	44.6
Communications/employee involvement	36.7	22.1
Family-care benefits	14.2	7.5
Union-management relations	26.6	12.4
Any functional area	75.4	60.4

Source: Estimates by the authors, based on data from the Human Resource Practices Survey.

for fewer than one-half of the HRPS respondents: the majority either did not engage in formal HR planning or evaluation, or if they did, did not consider them in their overall business planning (Figure 10). Large establishments were more likely to report integrating formal HR planning or evaluation into their overall business planning than small ones.

Job Design

How jobs are designed is an important element in the organization of the workplace. Practices in a number of other HRM areas, including training and compensation, are likely to follow from the job design.

We consider two aspects of job-design practice in Canadian industry. The first is the incidence of nontraditional designs. The second is the extent to which unionized, blue-collar workplaces – where traditional Taylorist job designs have been most deeply engrained – are moving away from the highly articulated job-classification structures that are so central to the industrial HRM model discussed in Chapter 1.

Nontraditional Job Designs

Job designs in workplaces built on Taylorist principles tend to be characterized by narrow and demarcated job definitions and specific

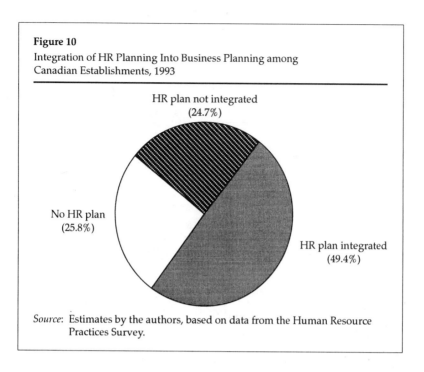

Figure 10
Integration of HR Planning Into Business Planning among
Canadian Establishments, 1993

HR plan not integrated
(24.7%)

No HR plan
(25.8%)

HR plan integrated
(49.4%)

Source: Estimates by the authors, based on data from the Human Resource
Practices Survey.

and unchanging employee assignments, with the worker's responsibility limited to his or her immediate job. A number of factors, most notably the diffusion of computer-based technologies, have called into question the effectiveness of this job design. Job designs in high-performance-workplace models, on the other hand, tend to have broad and flexible job definitions and often deploy workers anywhere within a family of jobs.

The HRPS asked respondents whether they had formally implemented nontraditional job designs based on job rotation, enlargement, enrichment, or self-directed work teams (Table 6). The results suggest that diffusion of these programs is limited, with the highest rates in electrical and electronic products and the lowest in fabricated metal products. Self-directed work teams are a more fundamental job-design innovation and were, not surprisingly, even less common than the other job designs.[4]

These nontraditional job designs are strongly associated with technological change. Among the establishments surveyed by the HRPS that introduced a significant amount of new technology between 1988

Table 6

Proportion of Establishments with Formal Job Design Programs, by Sector, 1993

Job design program	Wood products	Fabricated metal products	Electrical and electronic products	Selected business services	All sectors
			(Percent)		
Job rotation	31.5	17.7	29.8	13.7	22.5
Job enlargement	19.1	17.7	27.7	21.3	21.1
Job enrichment	19.7	15.1	30.5	22.3	21.4
Self-directed work teams	9.0	10.8	22.7	21.3	15.7
At least one program	38.2	29.6	46.8	36.0	37.0

Source: Estimates by the authors, based on data from the Human Resource Practices Survey.

and 1993, 41.5 percent indicated they had implemented at least one of the programs listed in Table 6; among the rest of the sample the figure was only 25.8 percent.

Trends in Job Classification

In many respects, the fluid job design of the high-performance workplace model runs counter to principles at the heart of the job-control unionism that has characterized Canadian industrial relations for much of this century. Some of the inherent conflicts include broad and flexible versus narrow and demarcated job definitions, compressed versus extended job-grade (i.e., pay) structures, and flexibility in assignments versus allocation by seniority (O'Grady 1994). These contradictions have taken on special significance as production has become increasingly computerized and oriented towards flexible specialization. While the traditional job designs are well suited to mass-production Taylorist workplaces, it is generally agreed that they are not well suited to the new production models.

In a study undertaken for the HRM Project, O'Grady (1994) examined job-classification trends over the past decade in unionized, industrial workplaces. The analysis is based on the contents of collective agreement job-classification clauses in force in 1981-83 and 1991-93 in 225 Ontario workplaces.[5] By comparing the same bargaining units over a 10-year period, O'Grady was able to observe how the 'articulation' of the job structure, i.e., the number of job grades and job definitions, has changed.[6]

This analysis leads to the conclusion that traditional job designs, i.e., those that are consistent with the industrial HRM model and job-control unionism, have remained dominant. O'Grady found that the highly articulated job structure of 1981-83[7] had changed very little by 1991-93. In both the number of job grades and job definitions, the increases and decreases over the period were roughly the same (Figure 11).

Two factors apparently underlie the persistence of traditional, highly articulated job designs. First, many firms did not seem motivated to institute changes: for example, where there had been extended job structures in 1981-83, O'Grady estimates that only one-quarter of the employers had chosen to move to more flexible structures by the early 1990s. Second, unions were often able to exert leverage which, in some cases, moderated or prevented employers' attempts to reduce the number of job classifications.

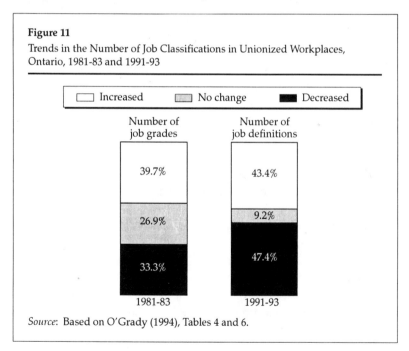

Figure 11
Trends in the Number of Job Classifications in Unionized Workplaces, Ontario, 1981-83 and 1991-93

Source: Based on O'Grady (1994), Tables 4 and 6.

Training

In recent years training has received more attention than any other HRM practice. Although there remain a number of important gaps in our knowledge, a general picture of workplace training in this country is emerging.

Incidence Rates

Estimates of the proportion of Canadian firms that train vary widely. These estimates, known as training 'incidence rates,' are extremely sensitive to definitions of what constitutes 'training' and to the characteristics of the firms being sampled.[8] To illustrate, the two most recent 'official' national surveys – the 1987 Human Resource Training and Development Survey and the 1991 National Training Survey – yield incidence rates of 31 and 70 percent, respectively.[9]

What conclusions can be drawn from results like these? The estimate of 70 percent by the National Training Survey indicates that most firms do undertake some structured training. However, the Human Resource Training and Development Survey and a number of other data sources suggest that only a minority of Canadian employers undertake *formal training designed to develop the vocational skills of their workers.*[10] In fact, as we will see below, the detailed results of the National Training Survey show that relatively little of the training reported can be considered formal, vocational skills training.

Three other points can be made about training activity in Canadian industry based on the surveys to date:

- Although the data tend to focus on formal training, most employer-based training is actually informal (Ekos Research Associates 1993a);
- Large firms are more likely to train than small ones, although the difference tends to be smaller when the definition of training is broadened to include informal or unstructured training (Betcherman 1993); and
- The large majority of firms do not take a systematic, forward-looking approach to training; roughly 20 percent appear to have a training budget and about 15 percent have a formal training plan (Canadian Labour Market and Productivity Centre 1993; Ekos Research Associates 1993a).

Types of Workplace Training

Training in the workplace can have a number of objectives, only some of which involve developing what economists call 'human capital' or the productive capabilities of employees. The National Training Survey collected a great deal of information about the types of training being undertaken in the workplace. A large portion involved training for purposes other than developing human capital (Canadian Labour Market and Productivity Centre 1993). For example, 26 percent of the training concerned health and safety and another 18 percent was for orientation. Training more closely linked to developing human capital – such as computer training and especially managerial, professional, and sales training and apprenticeships – was far less frequently reported.

The Human Resource Practices Survey also found a substantial amount of nonvocational training. Health and safety training was provided by 68 percent of the HRPS sample (Figure 12). As well, the data suggest that what is sometimes referred to as 'social' or 'cultural' training is quite prominent. About one-half of the respondents carried

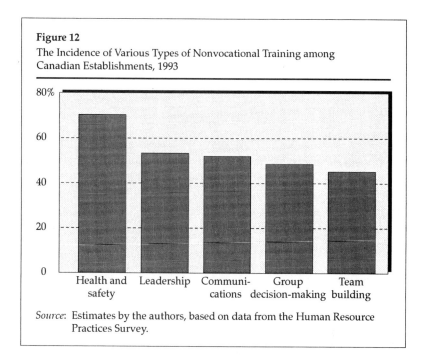

Figure 12

The Incidence of Various Types of Nonvocational Training among Canadian Establishments, 1993

Source: Estimates by the authors, based on data from the Human Resource Practices Survey.

out formal, structured training in each of the following areas: leader-
ship, communications, group decision-making, and team-building.

Training for New Technologies

Where Canadian firms are undertaking vocational or human-capital
oriented training, much of it appears to be driven by technological
change.[11] In a study conducted for the HRM Project, Caron (1993) used
the Working With Technology Survey (WWTS) to take a close look at
workplace training associated with the introduction of computer-
based technologies (CBT).

Her analysis suggests that computerization is creating a large and
growing demand for training. Between 1986 and 1991, 69.4 percent of
the establishments surveyed by the WWTS that had introduced CBT
reported that they had undertaken training to meet new skill requirements created by the technology. Overall, nearly 14,000 employees
participated in training, triple the number trained for CBT in the same
organizations during 1980-85.

Not only did computer-related training increase over the decade,
but there was also a major shift in who received it. While most workers
trained for the new computer technologies in the early 1980s were in
clerical occupations, the profile shifted dramatically toward managerial and professional/technical employees after 1985 (Figure 13). This
development reflects the ongoing diffusion of CBT and increasingly
sophisticated office applications.

Compensation

Standard compensation in Canadian workplaces has been based on
salaries or hourly wages. Pay rates have been dictated by some
combination of the level of responsibility, the significance of the job
or the job-holder, and market forces. While the standard practices still
predominate, alternative pay arrangements such as pay-for-
skill/knowledge, productivity gainsharing, and profit- sharing have
assumed a high profile in recent years. These plans are designed to
factor in the measured performance of the individual, work group, or
organization.

Such arrangements, known as 'variable,' 'performance-based,' or
'incentive-based' compensation, were reviewed by Chaykowski and
Lewis (1994) in a study carried out for the HRM Project. Their review
also makes the following points:

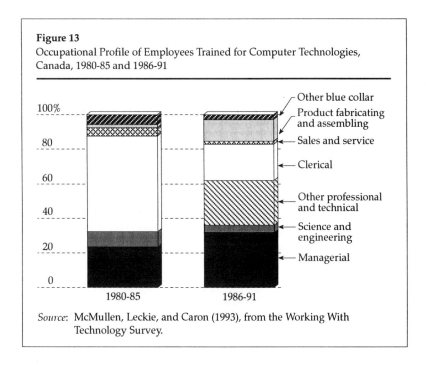

Figure 13
Occupational Profile of Employees Trained for Computer Technologies,
Canada, 1980-85 and 1986-91

Source: McMullen, Leckie, and Caron (1993), from the Working With
Technology Survey.

- Although often referred to as 'innovative,' variable-pay practices actually have a long history; the difference now is that they appear to be more common;
- The plans are frequently employer-initiated, usually because of their potential to increase performance by means of incentives and to more closely tie labour costs to business conditions; and
- Variable pay plans generally complement rather than replace standard wage and salary practices.

Chaykowski and Lewis note that much more is known about the diffusion of variable-pay practices in the US than in Canada. However, both the Human Resource Practices Survey and the Working With Technology Survey offer new empirical evidence on the situation in this country.

Incidence

Both surveys asked establishments whether they had implemented employee stock option plans (ESOPs), profit-sharing, productivity gainsharing, pay-for-skill/knowledge, or any other types of incentive-based pay system. The incidences reported by the two surveys were similar: 46.1 percent of the HRPS respondents and 43.3 percent of the WWTS respondents reported that they had some variable-pay arrangement (for nonmanagerial employees). As we discuss below, small firms have lower incidence rates. Because small firms are underrepresented in both samples, it is likely that these figures overestimate the economy-wide prevalence of variable-pay practices.

Table 7 presents the incidence of these variable-pay plans as reported to the HRPS and the WWTS. In both surveys, profit- sharing was most commonly reported. ESOPs and pay-for-skill/knowledge followed, and productivity gainsharing was the least common.

The WWTS panel data suggest that the incidence of variable-pay plans has increased somewhat in Canada. Restricting the analysis to the three types of plan included in both the 1985 and 1991 WWTS questionnaires (profit-sharing, productivity gainsharing, and pay-for-skill/knowledge), 37.1 percent of the establishments reported having at least one such arrangement in 1991, compared with 28.6 percent for the same establishments in 1985.[12]

The results of the WWTS and the HRPS show that the incidence of variable-pay practices is uneven among Canadian industries. The surveys provide the following picture of the diffusion patterns:

- The larger the establishment, the more likely it is to have implemented some form of variable-pay plan. According to the WWTS data, for example, only 26.5 percent of the establishments with fewer than 50 employees reported having implemented a variable-pay plan, compared with 50.6 percent of those with over 100 employees.
- Variable-pay practices are most frequently found in workplaces characterized by substantial technological change. Among establishments surveyed by the WWTS that introduced computer-based technology in both 1980-85 and 1986-91, 50.7 percent reported a variable-pay plan; the corresponding figure for establishments that introduced CBT in one period only (or not at all) was only 26.2 percent.[13]
- The diffusion of these plans has been greater among non-unionized than unionized establishments. The HRPS data, for example, reveal that the overall incidence is close to 50 percent higher in the absence of a union (Figure 14).[14] Of the particular

Table 7

Proportion of Establishments[1] with Selected Variable-Pay Practices, 1991 and 1993

Variable pay practice	Working with Technology Survey, 1991	Human Resource Practices Survey, 1993
	(Percent)	
Profit-sharing	18.2	21.6
ESOPs[2]	13.1	14.1
Pay-for-skill/knowledge	6.0	14.5
Productivity gainsharing	5.0	6.5
Other incentive pay[3]	11.2	6.4

Source: Estimates by the authors, based on data from the Working with Technology Survey (WWTS) and the Human Resource Practices Survey (HRPS).

[1] Only establishments reporting plans that included nonmanagerial employees.
[2] Employee stock option plans.
[3] Refers to the categories 'other incentive-based pay system' and 'small group incentive plans' in the WWTS and HRPS, respectively.

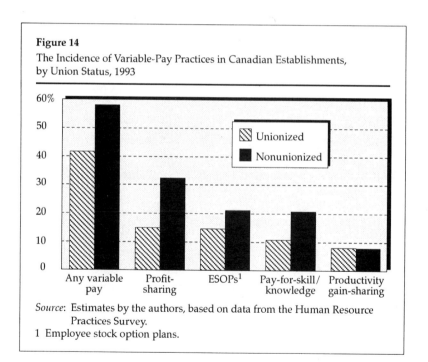

Figure 14

The Incidence of Variable-Pay Practices in Canadian Establishments, by Union Status, 1993

Source: Estimates by the authors, based on data from the Human Resource Practices Survey.
1 Employee stock option plans.

variable-pay practices covered by the HRPS, union status matters for all except productivity gainsharing. The negative assoication between variable-pay practices and unionization supports the perception that unions sometimes oppose these plans because they transfer risk from the employer to the worker and because they could promote speed-ups and competition among workers.

Sustainability

How sustainable are variable pay and other HR practices generally? When firms introduce nontraditional programs, do they 'stick,' or is there a high failure rate? With the longitudinal WWTS database, this issue can be addressed directly by looking at whether respondents reporting a practice in 1985 still reported it in 1991.

As above, we restricted our analysis of the sustainability of variable-pay practices to the three types of plan included in both years covered by the WWTS (1985 and 1991): profit-sharing, pay-for-skill/knowledge, and productivity gainsharing.[15] Among establishments reporting one of these in 1985, 72 percent also reported one in 1991. In other words, a fair proportion of variable-pay practices were *not* sustained over the six-year period. Observable firm characteristics such as size, sector, union status, and age did not affect the sustainability to any significant degree.

To gain more insight into why programs did not stick, follow-up phone interviews were carried out with establishments that reported dropping variable-pay plans. Most gave economic reasons, especially that there were no profits or productivity gains to share.[16]

Employee Participation

Traditionally, North American workplaces have not encouraged the participation of employees in decisions about the operations of their work area or the organization more broadly. An important criticism of the traditional models has been this lack of employee involvement. Since the 1970s, employers have experimented with an alphabet soup of initiatives designed, at least in part, to change this. Often inspired by Japanese management methods, these initiatives include quality-of-working-life (QWL), quality circles (QCs), employee involvement (EI), and total quality management (TQM).

Both the Human Resource Practices Survey and the Working With Technology Survey collected information on the experience of Canadian establishments regarding employee participation. In each case, respondents were asked to report only on *formal* programs. As with variable-pay practices, the surveys paint a consistent picture with respect to employee-participation practices.

Incidence

Slightly less than half the respondents to the two surveys reported that they had a formal employee-participation program: the rates were 43.1 percent in the HRPS sample and 47.5 percent in the WWTS sample. (The underrepresentation in both surveys of small firms, where these programs have a low incidence, has undoubtedly led to an upward bias in the estimates.)

Has the diffusion of employee-participation programs grown in recent years? Our data suggest there have been modest increases, but nothing dramatic. Among the respondents in the WWTS longitudinal panel, 42.9 percent reported some formal employee participation activity in 1985, compared with 47.5 percent in 1991.[17]

The incidence of employee-participation programs varies according to selected establishment characteristics (Table 8). Large establishments are more likely to report them than small ones. They are also more frequently found in workplaces characterized by technological change. And the incidence is somewhat higher in establishments where a union is present, although the difference is not significant.[18]

Issues Dealt With

Employee-participation initiatives can deal with a range of issues and many cover more than one. The most common are quality and health and safety (Figure 15). The former is consistent with all of the attention that has been paid to quality in recent years, while the latter reflects the requirement in many jurisdictions that labour-management health and safety committees be instituted.

Sustainability

Of WWTS respondents reporting the presence of a formal program in 1985, 67 percent indicated that one was still in place in 1991 (Betcherman, Leckie, and Verma 1994). Although there are no obvious benchmarks, this statistic suggests a relatively high failure rate in that one

Table 8

Proportion of Establishments with Employee-Participation Programs, by
Selected Establishment Characteristics, 1993

Characteristic	Employee-participation program
	(Percent)
Number of employees***	
1-49	35.8
50-99	36.2
100-249	51.5
250+	59.2
Technology[1]***	
Significant change	46.4
No significant change	35.0
Union status	
Unionized	46.3
Nonunionized	40.7
All establishments	43.1

Source: Estimates by the authors, based on data from the Human Resource
Practices Survey.

[1] Based on whether the respondent identified significant changes in
production/operation technologies over the preceding five years (1988-1993).
*** The differences are statistically significant at the .01 level.

Figure 15

Issues Covered by Employee Participation Programs among
Canadian Establishments, 1993

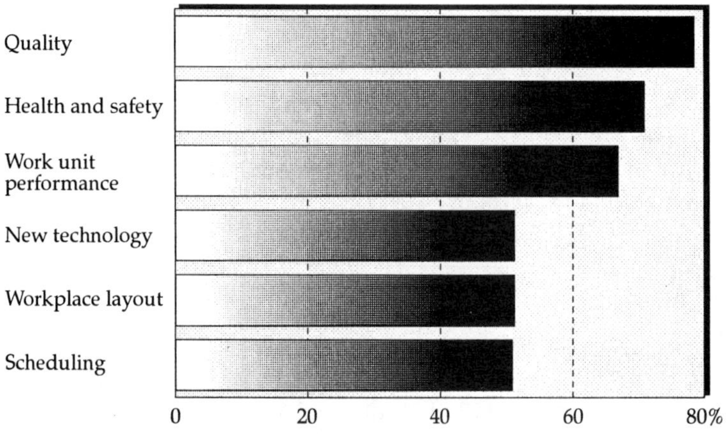

Source: Estimates by the authors, based on data from the Human Resource
Practices Survey.

establishment in three had dropped its program. No particular organizational characteristics such as sector, age, size, or union status were statistically significant determinants of sustainability.

Establishments reporting that they had dropped a formal employee-participation program between 1985 and 1991 were contacted to find out why. The reason given most often was that the program was a victim of downsizing or restructuring. This suggests that, for some firms, this type of initiative is viewed more as a 'frill' than as a serious initiative to enhance firm performance.

Flexible Scheduling and Family-Care Policies

As a result of the growing participation of women in the labour force, especially women with children at home, pressure has been growing for changes in scheduling and for benefits relating to family care. Some firms are finding that if they want to retain valued employees[19] and avoid the negative consequences of workers encountering problems balancing job and family responsibilities, they must respond to this pressure.

Alternative Scheduling

Despite evidence that work and family pressure is growing, the HRPS found that close to 60 percent of respondents did not offer alternative scheduling arrangements to their employees (Table 9). The incidence of these arrangements (and family-care benefits) is closely related to the number of female employees and their bargaining power. For example, the majority of establishments in the business-services sector offered alternative scheduling; of the sectors surveyed, business services has the largest share of female employees and substantial female representation in the professional and technical occupations. Alternative scheduling was least likely to be found in the wood and the fabricated metal products sectors, both of which are characterized by traditional, male employment profiles.

By far the most common alternative scheduling arrangement was flexible working hours. Only small percentages of respondents offered other arrangements such as a compressed work week, work-at-home, or job-sharing. All types of alternative scheduling arrangements were more common in the largest establishments (250 or more employees) and in nonunionized establishments.

Table 9

Proportion of Establishments Offering Various Alternative Scheduling Arrangements, by Sector, 1993

Scheduling arrangement	Wood products	Fabricated metal products	Electrical and electronic products	Selected business services	All sectors
			(Percent)		
Flexible working hours	15.8	17.7	35.0	56.7	31.8
Compressed work week	17.5	8.6	14.0	13.4	13.6
Work at home	5.6	4.8	9.8	16.6	9.2
Job sharing	6.2	3.8	9.1	9.6	7.1
Other arrangements	3.4	0.5	1.4	4.8	2.6
None of the above	67.2	72.0	53.8	36.4	57.0

Source: Estimates by the authors, based on data from the Human Resource Practices Survey.

Family-Care Benefits

Only 42 percent of the HRPS respondents reported that they provided benefits that explicitly address personal/family-care needs (Figure 16). More commonly provided were employee-assistance programs which, as a general rule, do not address personal/family-care needs *per se* but deal with such issues as substance abuse and mental-health counselling. Explicit provision of daycare and eldercare benefits was essentially nonexistent in all sectors.

As might be expected, the provision of personal/family-care benefits increased with establishment size. For example, maternity/parental leave or benefits (beyond those required by law) were in place in 29.0 percent of the largest establishments, but in only 6.7 percent of the smallest ones. Similarly, only 16.8 percent of establishments with fewer than 50 employees had an employee-assistance program, whereas 74.3 percent of the largest establishments (more than 250 employees) had one.

There was very little difference between the incidence of such benefits in unionized and nonunionized establishments, with one exception. Employee-assistance programs were found in 45.7 percent of unionized establishments, but in only 28.8 percent of nonunionized ones.

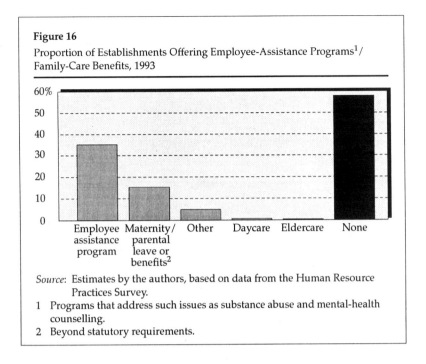

Figure 16

Proportion of Establishments Offering Employee-Assistance Programs[1]/
Family-Care Benefits, 1993

Source: Estimates by the authors, based on data from the Human Resource
Practices Survey.
1 Programs that address such issues as substance abuse and mental-health
counselling.
2 Beyond statutory requirements.

Use of Nonstandard Employment

Most of the new jobs created in recent years have been nonstandard:
part-time, short-term, and temporary agency work, and independent
contractors.[20] In 1992 approximately 30 percent of those employed
occupied nonstandard jobs.

It is widely believed that this phenomenon is being driven by
changes in the composition of the labour force and by the growth of
service industries. In fact, these factors have had only a small impact
on the overall prevalence of nonstandard employment in Canada.[21]
Instead, since the early 1980s, the incidence of nonstandard employment has risen significantly among both men and women, in all age
groups, and in all major industry groups. This suggests that broader
systemic factors have been the dominant influence.

One theory is that many employers, largely in response to increased
competition, have attempted to minimize their labour costs and enhance their flexibility by reducing their 'core' workforces – traditional,
full-time, permanent employees – and have compensated by hiring
nonstandard, or contingent, workers on an as-needed basis.[22] This, it

is argued, has been reinforced during the past two recessions when the need to cut costs has been heightened. This theory dovetails with both the rising incidence of nonstandard employment and the extensive downsizing observed among Canadian employers during the past decade. Interviews conducted with employers as part of this study provide broad confirmation of this theory.

Patterns of Nonstandard Work Arrangements

Within the HRPS sample, the overwhelming majority of establishments (87 percent) reported at least one type of nonstandard work arrangement; 35 percent used all four. Short-term/temporary work was the most prevalent, followed by part-time work and independent contracting (Table 10). Further, the use of each of these employment forms, especially independent contracting, increased between 1988 and 1993. Temporary-agencies were the least-used nonstandard work form; it was reported by half of the HRPS respondents and its use decreased over the period.

Table 10

Proportion of Establishments Employing Various Types of Nonstandard Workers, by Selected Establishment Characteristics, 1993

Characteristic	Part time	Short-term temporary	Temporary agency	Independent contractors
		(Percent)		
Sector				
Wood products	73.7	74.5	28.6	61.3
Fabricated metal products	49.7	54.6	37.7	47.2
Electrical and electronic products	64.1	68.7	60.9	61.6
Selected business services	84.5	87.9	73.7	69.4
Number of employees				
1-49	60.9	64.6	40.0	50.8
50-99	67.9	71.7	46.2	51.2
100-249	69.7	73.9	53.7	69.1
250+	77.9	76.8	67.7	76.5
Region				
Atlantic	79.2	87.5	43.5	60.9
Quebec	56.8	66.2	34.1	39.1
Ontario	67.7	69.2	58.0	63.3
Prairies	75.6	81.2	55.4	66.7
BC	77.6	74.8	50.5	72.9
All establishments	68.5	71.8	50.5	59.9

Source: Estimates by the authors, based on data from the Human Resource Practices Survey.

There were significant differences among sectors in the pattern of use. Establishments in business services made by far the heaviest use of every category of nonstandard work, while the fabricated metal products industry made the least use of it.

Reasons for the Use of Nonstandard Workers

The desire for greater flexibility seems to be the reason for much of the use of nonstandard workers. The most common reasons cited by HRPS respondents were to cope with irregular business levels and to temporarily augment the workforce. This was especially the case with short-term/temporary workers. The most common motive for employing workers part time was because there was insufficient work for full-time positions. Independent contractors were most often used for special projects, while temporary agency personnel were most often used to cover for absent workers.

While cited less often than the desire for flexibility, the need to control labour costs was also an important reason among many establishments using nonstandard workers; it was cited by between 22 and 29 percent of establishments employing part-time, short-term/temporary workers, and independent contractors.[23]

The fact that employees wanted to work part time was an important reason cited for the use of part-time workers; it was given by over one-quarter of the establishments using them. This was not a major factor, however, in explaining the use of other nonstandard work forms, which tended to be largely employer-driven.

HRM Systems[24]

In this section, we shift the focus from individual HRM practices viewed in isolation to the complete set of practices within the firm – in other words, its HRM *system*. Using the Human Resource Practices Survey data, we show how practices tend to cluster together at the firm level into a few distinct patterns.

Associations Among HR Practices

The HRPS contains information on a wide range of HRM practices in a large number of firms. As such, it offers a unique database for analysing how individual practices fit together to form HRM systems. We isolated 12 firm-level variables to measure whether:

- A formal employee-participation program exists;
- A formal job-design program exists;
- A variable-pay arrangement exists for nonmanagerial employees;
- Employer-sponsored vocational-skills training has involved at least 50 percent of employees in the past year;
- Employer-sponsored nonvocational, or 'cultural,' training (for group problem-solving/decision-making, team-building, or communications) has been undertaken in the past year;
- Job vacancies are typically filled by internal promotion (rather than by external hiring);
- Merit enters into the promotion process (as opposed to exclusive reliance on seniority);
- At least some employees regularly work under an alternative scheduling arrangement;
- Family-care benefits are offered;
- A comprehensive fringe-benefit plan exists;[25]
- Wages and benefits are considered to be above the industry average; and
- Formal human-resource planning exists and is integrated into overall business planning.

The point underlying our interest in HRM systems – that individual practices are linked – is illustrated by the high degree of statistical correlation among practices at the firm level. Table 11 presents the pair-wise correlation coefficients for the 12 HR practices listed above.[26] Of the 66 correlations describing the associations between these practices, 65 are positive, and 49 of these are statistically significant at least at the .10 level. What this means is that firms tend either to have many of these practices or very few of them.

Identifying Distinct HRM Systems

These strong correlations suggest that there are quite distinct patterns of HRM practices among firms. In order to identify groups of establishments with common sets of HRM practices, cluster analysis was applied to the HRPS data.[27]

The analysis revealed three different clusters. The first includes firms reporting very few of the 12 HRM practices; this model, which we call *traditional*, places a low strategic priority on human resources. The other two are much more active and give HRM practices higher

Table 11

Correlation Coefficients[1] Among Selected Human-Resource Practices, 1993

HR practice	1	2	3	4	5	6	7	8	9	10	11
1 Employee participation											
2 Job design	.201***										
3 Variable pay	.178***	.183***									
4 'High' training	.145***	.032	.095**								
5 'Group' training	.328***	.172***	.202***	.223***							
6 Internal promotion	.060	.104***	.084	.098***	.064*						
7 Merit promotion	.014	-.060	.044	.036	.075**	.012					
8 Flexible scheduling	.082*	.141***	.178***	.053	.163***	.086**	.141***				
9 Family-care benefits	.244***	.193***	.097***	.170***	.320***	.161***	.111***	.139***			
10 'High' benefits	.097***	.061	.052	.065*	.113***	.007	.051	.065*	.234***		
11 'High' wages	.071*	.093**	.135***	.089*	.064*	.048	.017	.040	.100***	.026	
12 HR in business plan	.202***	.230***	.129***	.165***	.320***	.157***	.076*	.184***	.235***	.100	.083

Source: Estimates by the authors, based on data from the Human Resource Practices Survey.

*The correlation coefficient is significant at the .01 level.
**The correlation coefficient is significant at the .05 level.
***The correlation coefficient is significant at the .10 level.

strategic value. They are similar in terms of their emphasis on human resources, but they use somewhat different practices to achieve their objectives. One includes establishments that focus on extrinsic rewards and incentives, including variable pay, internal promotion, and high wages and benefits; we call this model *compensation-based*. The other, which we call *participation-based*, includes firms that rely on job quality and intrinsic rewards and emphasize employee participation and job design.

The patterns of individual HRM practices characterizing each of these clusters are summarized in Figure 17.

Profiles of the HRM Clusters

The HRPS data suggest that the traditional HRM system, which places a low strategic priority on human resources, remains the standard. In fact, the majority of establishments in the sample (53 percent) use this system (Figure 18, Panel A). The more strategic and active models – the compensation– and participation-based systems – describe much smaller groups, representing 23 and 24 percent of the respondents, respectively.

Figure 17
Incidence[1] of Human Resource Practices among
Establishments in HRM Clusters, 1993

	HRM cluster		
	Traditional	Compensation	Participation
Employee participation	L	M	H
Job design	L	M	H
Variable pay	L	H	M
"High" training	L	H	H
"Group" training	L	H	H
Internal promotion	M	H	M
Merit promotion	M	H	L
Flexible scheduling	L	H	L
Family benefits	L	H	H
"High" benefits	L	H	L
"High" wages	M	H	L
HR in business plan	L	H	H

Source: Estimates by the authors, based on data from the Human Resource
          Practices Survey.
1 "H" indicates high relative incidence, "M" medium relative incidence, and
   "L" low relative incidence.

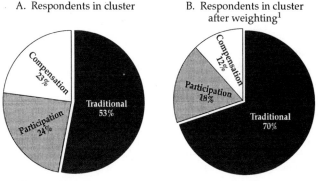

Figure 18
Distribution of Establishments into HRM Clusters,
With and Without Weighting, 1993

A. Respondents in cluster

B. Respondents in cluster after weighting[1]

Source: Estimates by the authors, based on data from the Human Resource Practices Survey.
1 The sample results were weighted using Statistics Canada establishment-count data on establishment size (number of employees) in each of the four sectors that were surveyed for the HRPS.

As we will see below, the incidence of these three systems differs according to various organizational characteristics. One particularly important factor is size, which is strongly associated with the traditional model. Since the HRPS underrepresents small establishments, we have reestimated the proportion of firms in each cluster after weighting the sample so that it reflects the actual size distributions in the four sectors included in the HRPS. As would be expected, the result is an even stronger presence of the traditional system; with the weighting adjustments the incidence of this model is 70 percent (Figure 18, Panel B).

Environmental Factors

Table 12 shows how the external business environment has been changing for the three HRM clusters. In some respects, the environmental pressures are similar for all three; this is particularly the case for greater competition, which was the change most frequently cited in all three clusters. However, there are some important differences. Establishments in the traditional cluster were significantly less likely

Table 12

Proportion of Establishments Reporting Significant Changes in the External
Business Environment in 1988-93, by HRM Cluster

| | HRM cluster | | |
Change	Traditional	Compensation	Participation
	(Percent)		
Greater competition	77.0	83.0	78.0
Regulatory requirements**	66.0	74.0	76.0
Technology***	61.0	68.0	74.0
Foreign-market orientation	49.0	53.0	55.0
Senior management***	43.0	56.0	60.0
Product or service	40.0	42.0	43.0
Controlling ownership	33.0	37.0	39.0

Source: Estimates by the authors, based on data from the Human Resource Practices
Survey.

** The differences are statistically significant at the .05 level.
*** The differences are statistically significant at the .01 level.

to report either major technological change or new senior management than were those in the participation-based and, to a lesser
degree, the compensation-based clusters. Finally, for all of the items
included in Table 12, establishments in the traditional HRM cluster
were least likely to report significant change, which suggests that
these firms have been (or perceive themselves to have been) less
affected by environmental change than those in the other two clusters.

Organizational Characteristics

Table 13 profiles the establishments in each HRM cluster by sector,
size, and union status. In all the sectors covered in the HRPS, the
traditional model is the most common. However, while it is clearly
the norm in the wood products and fabricated metal products industries, it is somewhat less dominant in electrical and electronic products, where the participation-based system has a relatively high
incidence, or in business services, where the compensation-based
approach is more common than in the other sectors. The traditional
model is most prevalent among small firms, and the more strategic
approaches become increasingly common as establishment size increases. Among establishments with 250 employees or more, 54
percent fall into the compensation-based cluster. Finally, the distribu-

Table 13

Distribution of Establishments by HRM Cluster, by Selected Establishment Characteristics, 1993.

Characteristic	HRM cluster			Total
	Traditional	Compensation	Participation	
	(Percent[1])			
Sector***				
Wood products	61.0	19.0	20.0	100.0
Fabricated metal products	65.0	15.0	20.0	100.0
Electrical and electronic products	43.0	22.0	35.0	100.0
Selected business services	41.0	36.0	24.0	100.0
Number of employees***				
1-49	70.0	12.0	17.0	100.0
50-99	61.0	18.0	21.0	100.0
100-249	44.0	25.0	31.0	100.0
250+	18.0	54.0	28.0	100.0
Union status				
Unionized	49.0	23.0	27.0	100.0
Non unionized	55.0	24.0	22.0	100.0
All establishments***	53.0	23.0	24.0	100.0

Source: Estimates by the authors, based on data from the Human Resource Practices Survey.

[1] Numbers may not sum to 100 because of rounding.
*** The differences are statistically significant at the .01 level.

tions of unionized and nonunionized establishments by HRM system are quite similar.

Business Strategy

The elements of business strategies reported by the HRPS respondents in each HRM system are summarized in Table 14. There are some differences: for example, the most frequently cited strategic element in the traditional cluster was reducing nonlabour costs; in the compensation-based and participation-based clusters it was increasing employee skill levels. However, most notable is that every strategic element other than those involving cost was most frequently cited by the participation-based cluster, followed by the compensation-based one, and least often cited by the traditional cluster.

Modelling HRM-System Choice

Going beyond pure description of the types of establishments in each group, we modelled HRM-system choice, considering the joint effects

Table 14

Proportion of Establishments Reporting Various Elements in their Business Strategies, by HRM Cluster, 1993.

Elements	HRM cluster		
	Traditional	Compensation	Participation
	(Percent)		
Reducing operating(non-labour) costs*	74.0	74.0	83.0
Increasing employees' skill levels***	64.0	85.0	88.0
Developing new products/ markets*	66.0	72.0	74.0
Reducing labour costs	66.0	64.0	73.0
Introducing new technology***	60.0	66.0	78.0
Reorganizing the work process***	50.0	62.0	78.0
Enhancing labour-management cooperation***	40.0	56.0	66.0
Undertaking R&D***	37.0	43.0	52.0

Source: Estimates by the authors, based on data from the Human Resource Practices Survey.

* The differences are statistically significant at the .10 level.
*** The differences are statistically significant at the .01 level.

of a number of potential determinants. This modelling exercise took the form of a logistic regression for each HRM cluster, where the probability of an establishment being in that cluster is calculated as a function of the following variables: sector, number of employees, union status, change in the environment, business strategy, and region.[28] The results of these regressions are summarized in Table 15.[29]

From this analysis, the following observations emerge about HRM-system choice:

- The goods industries differ from business services.[30] This is particularly true for the wood products and the fabricated metal products industries, which represent the 'old-economy' industries in the HRPS sample. They are positively associated with traditional HRM approaches and negatively with either of the more strategic workplace models.
- Size is also an important determinant of HRM-system choice. The regressions consistently show that the larger the establishment, the more likely it is to have moved away from a traditional model, most typically to a compensation-based one.

Table 15

Estimated Impact of Selected Establishment Characteristics on Probability of Choosing Each HRM Cluster,[1] 1993

	HRM cluster		
Characteristic	Traditional	Compensation	Participation
		(Percent)	
Sector (relative to Selected business services)			
Wood products	31	-17	-11
Fabricated metal products	30	-12	-15
Electrical and electronic products	-	-12	-
Number of employees (relative to 50-99)			
1-49	-	-	-
100-249	-17	10	-
250+	-46	31	-
Union present (relative to no union)	-	-	8
Number of environmental changes	-	2	-
Business strategy[2]			
'Process'	-15	4	11
'Cost'	-	-	4
'Product'	-	-	-
Prediction rate	79	77	72
Number of observations	597	597	597

Source: Estimates by the authors, based on data from the Human Resource Practices Survey.

[1] Calculated as the impact of the variable on the probability of being in the selected group at the mean value of the variable. The impact is only calculated where regression coefficients are significant at the .10 level or more. Region is also controlled for in all of the equations. The full regression results on which this table is based are in Appendix C3.
[2] Variable values are factor scores for each strategy.

- Unionization is associated with the participation-based approach while nonunionized status is associated with the traditional system.[31]
- Changes in the organizational environment do not appear to have a major impact on HRM-system choice, once other factors are taken into account.[32] This does not mean that the environment does not matter, but rather that the environmental pressures, especially growing competition, are affecting virtually everyone.
- Business strategy affects HRM-system choice. The strongest impact involves 'process-oriented' strategies that focus on the operational process within the firm. The presence of this strategy

increases the probability of adopting a participation-based and to a lesser extent a compensation-based approach to human resource management, while significantly decreasing the probability of adopting a traditional approach.

Summary

Clearly some Canadian firms are moving towards a high-performance workplace model. Our analysis suggests that, among these organizations, two variations of this model are being pursued. One focuses on enhancing employee participation and job quality, and the other emphasizes compensation incentives.

However, our evidence indicates that the large majority of Canadian firms still follow traditional approaches to human resource management. Despite the environmental pressures, these organizations are maintaining Taylorist job designs, making low investments in employee training, not integrating human resources into strategic planning, not involving employees, and not responding to their employees' needs for more family-friendly policies. Traditional HRM systems are most prevalent in older industries and among small firms.

Notes

[1] While our surveys were designed to get a broad perspective on HRM practices in Canada, the limitations of the samples should be noted. They do not cover the public or quasi-public sectors, and they underrepresent very small firms and those in certain service industries such as retail trade, accommodation and food, and personal services.

[2] The capital-investment case was included to provide a benchmark for the HR-related decisions. The hypothetical case put to respondents concerned who would make the final decision about an increase of 20 percent in capital-equipment investments.

[3] This does not preclude the possibility that the HR people can play an important consultative or advisory role, even though the ultimate decision might be made elsewhere.

[4] In fact, teams often incorporate job rotation, enlargement, or enrichment into their designs.

[5] Almost 90 percent of the workplaces sampled were in manufacturing, with the remainder scattered through the resource and services sectors.

[6] In addition to analysing the contracts, O'Grady asked managers in 101 of these workplaces about their perceptions of the reorganization of job structures and the extent of union resistance. More details on the methodol-

ogy are available in O'Grady (1994).

⁷ For example, O'Grady characterized the number of job (i.e., pay) grades as 'moderately extended' (11-20 grades) or 'highly' extended (over 20 grades) in 74 percent of the workplaces.

⁸ For more details on methodological issues associated with estimating employer-based training, see OECD (1991).

⁹ Although employer-based training may well have increased in this period, it is likely that the gap in these rates primarily reflects different definitions. The 1987 survey counted training firms as those reporting training with 'an identifiable structured plan and objectives designed to develop a worker's skill and competence' (Rechnitzer 1990). The 1991 survey used a broader definition that included organizations that participated in one or more of the following: spending money directly related to training employees; providing tuition or time off for courses; including training responsibilities in the job description of any employees; purchasing or leasing equipment where supplier service included training; and having employees in apprenticeship, internship, or co-op programs (Canadian Labour Market and Productivity Centre 1993).

¹⁰ Incidence rates from a number of national surveys through the 1980s are consistent with this conclusion. See Betcherman (1993) for a list of these. More recent supporting evidence can be found in a 1992 nationwide survey by Ekos Research Associates (1993a), where 28.3 percent of the responding organizations reported some formal training during the preceding year.

¹¹ For example, the National Training Survey data reveal that computer training for office and nonoffice equipment accounted for 18 percent of the total training hours, more than any other vocational category (Canadian Labour Market and Productivity Centre 1993).

¹² ESOPs and 'other' incentive-pay systems were included only in the later questionnaire. Unlike the other statistics presented on variable pay, these incidence rates over time include all plans covering managers and non-managers. For more details on variable pay in the WWTS sample, see Betcherman, Leckie, and Verma (1994).

¹³ The relationship between technological change, on the one hand, and variable pay and employee participation, on the other, is explored in Betcherman, McMullen, and Leckie (1994). Using regression analysis, they find that the level of computer-based technologies is significantly associated with each of these practices, independent of other establishment characteristics.

¹⁴ Moreover, the contents of collective agreements suggest that variable-pay plans are not becoming more prevalent in the unionized sector. Tracking wage-related clauses in major Canadian contracts between 1987 and 1993, Chaykowski and Lewis (1994) found no significant change in the incidence of variable-pay arrangements.

¹⁵ This analysis is reported in more detail in Betcherman, Leckie, and Verma (1994).

[16] Of the 11 companies that participated in this follow-up, seven gave this as the primary reason.

[17] Note that there were some differences in the wording of the questions on employee participation in the two WWTS questionnaires. See Betcherman, Leckie, and Verma (1994).

[18] Regression analysis based on the WWTS data indicates that union status is not a significant determinant of whether an establishment has an employee participation program. See Betcherman, McMullen, and Leckie (1994).

[19] Some female professionals in career positions, for example, have been able to negotiate alternative scheduling arrangements and still retain their 'good' jobs. In their survey, Duxbury and Higgins (1994) find that 5.4 percent of women in managerial and professional occupations were working part-time in 1993. That percentage was 10.6 percent among women in 'earner' occupations–clerical, administrative, technical, retail, or production workers.

[20] Short-term jobs are defined as those lasting less than six months. Independent contracting is work done on a self-employed basis by people who do not themselves have employees.

[21] While a rising participation rate among women did contribute to the growth of nonstandard work during the 1980s, this contribution was almost exactly offset by the negative impact of the shrinking youth labour force share occasioned by declining numbers of young people. On the demand side, changes in industrial structure had a minimal impact on the incidence of nonstandard employment, explaining only 6 percent of the increase during the 1980s. For a more extensive discussion, see Economic Council of Canada (1991).

[22] Core workers are typically viewed as those with a long-term attachment to their employers, a degree of job stability, some prospects for advancement, and compensation that typically includes a benefit package. Contingent workers, on the other hand, generally have no long-term employer attachment, no implicit expectation of career advancement, little job security, and no access to benefit packages.

[23] These findings are supported by interviews conducted for this analysis, in which employers cited increased flexibility and reduced labour costs as the major advantages of nonstandard employment. Less control over the workforce is viewed as the major disadvantage of nonstandard workforms other than permanent part-time work.

[24] This section is based on a background paper prepared for the Human Resource Management Project by Leckie (1994).

[25] A comprehensive benefits plan was defined as having at least six of the following (for nonmanagerial employees): pension plan, extended medical insurance, dental insurance, paid sick leave, long-term disability insurance, supplementary unemployment benefits, and supplementary maternity benefits.

[26] Each practice was measured as a binary variable, with a value of 1 where it exists and 0 where it does not.

[27] Cluster analysis assigns establishments to clusters so that the variation within clusters is minimized and the separation among clusters is maximized. For more details, see Leckie (1994).

[28] The change-in-environment variable is specified as the number of significant environmental changes reported by the establishment from a list of seven asked about in the survey. The strategy variables are operationalized as the establishment factor scores for the three business-strategy types – process-, cost-, and product-oriented. These emerged as the principal factors in a factor analysis of the HRPS responses on business strategy. For more details on these, see Chapter 2. The region variable coefficients are not reported.

[29] For details on the methodology, see Leckie (1994).

[30] Business services is the variable omitted from the industry set, and the figures for the other sectors should be interpreted as their impact relative to that for business services. Similarly, the size-variable impact is measured relative to the 50-99 employees size-category and the union impact is relative to nonunionized status.

[31] This finding that unionization is assoicated with participation-based HRM is consistent with the findings of much of the existing research. See, for example, Eaton and Voos (1992).

[32] In an alternative specification, the types of environmental change, rather than the amount of change, were included. However, none of these specific changes were statistically significant determinants of HRM-system choice.

4

The Links Between Human Resource Management and Firm Performance

Does human resource management really matter? Do 'high-performance' workplace models actually lead to high-performance workplaces? Much of the current interest in HRM revolves around questions like these. Certainly, for managers and practitioners who are looking for answers in today's competitive environment, the implications of HRM choices for the performance of their organization is *the* question.

In this chapter, we focus on the link between HRM practices and firm performance. This has been a difficult relationship to disentangle because of a number of methodological problems. Very recently, however, researchers have started to gain some insight into the impact of different HRM approaches on firm performance. We begin by reviewing these findings, which are based exclusively on US surveys. We then present new analysis using Canadian data from the Human Resource Practices Survey (HRPS) and a survey of companies in the Atlantic provinces.

What Do We Already Know?

Interest in the relationship between human resource management and firm performance has been sparked by the spread of nontraditional practices. As these have received more attention, questions have inevitably been raised about whether they actually pay off.

Serious research on the HRM-firm performance link has only just begun, however. And, while there is growing evidence that certain HRM approaches are associated with positive outcomes, the case is by no means clear cut, partly because the analysis presents tough methodological challenges.

Methodological Issues

The ideal research design would permit a calculation of how different firm-level HRM approaches affect firm performance while controlling for other factors that might influence those performance outcomes. Unfortunately, methodological and data problems crop up at each stage of the analysis.

First, few databases really capture the HRM approach within the firm. Consequently, much of the research has been limited to estimating the effects of individual practices. The second problem involves measuring firm performance: while employers and practitioners are primarily interested in what affects the financial bottom-line, researchers often have little choice but to use 'intermediate' indicators like productivity or quality, and often even these are far from precise. Third, firm performance (especially financial performance) can be affected by a wide range of factors, which makes it difficult to isolate the impact of HRM. Finally, even where associations can be established between HRM systems and performance, the causal links are difficult to identify; in other words, do certain practices lead to successful organizations or do successful organizations adopt certain practices?

Research Findings

In a review of the literature on the HRM-firm performance relationship for the Human Resource Management Project, Weber (1994) finds mixed evidence. She focused on six different functional areas and found that in some, there is either weak or nonexistent support for performance effects (e.g., HR planning) or not enough research to draw any conclusions (e.g., training). In others, including variable pay and employee participation, she found a growing body of research demonstrating favourable performance impacts. In fact, Weber concludes that '[e]vidence in favour of the positive productivity effects of participative programs, including participative compensation systems, is nearly at a critical mass stage. ...'

Certainly this is the conclusion drawn by the US Department of Labor (1993) in its evaluation of recent research. The department reviewed 29 studies of employee participation; of these, 14 found positive productivity effects, 13 had ambiguous results, and only two identified negative effects. It assessed variable-pay practices similarly favourably, specifically profit-sharing and productivity gainsharing.

Focusing on HRM Systems

Although most studies have addressed the performance question by focusing on the impact of individual practices, a more promising approach is from the vantage point of the set of practices, or the HRM system, within the firm. There are two reasons for focusing on human resource management as a system. First, as we saw in Chapter 3, there are strong correlations at the firm level among different practices, with the result that there are quite distinct HRM clusters. Second, it is only from the perspective of the system that the complementarities among practices can be captured.

Some very recent American research suggests that the performance effects of HRM are clearer and stronger when systems rather than individual practices are considered. Moreover, these studies, using very different methodologies, find significant relationships between firm performance and 'high-performance' workplace models. The following abstracts of this research illustrate these points:

- Conducting a 'meta-analysis' of 131 field studies of organizational innovation, Macy, Bliese, and Norton (1991) found that the innovations led to positive financial outcomes reflected in lower costs and higher quality and output. They also observed 'behavioral' outcomes, including lower turnover and absenteeism. In general, more comprehensive workplace reform led to more favourable outcomes than did piecemeal change.
- MacDuffie and Krafcik (1992), using data from 62 automobile factories, found that 'flexible production' plants (with many elements of the 'high-performance' workplace model) performed significantly better in terms of production time and defect rates than 'mass production' plants (those operating under a traditional HRM approach).
- In the most rigorous evaluation to date, Ichniowski, Shaw, and Prennushi (1993) examined the HRM-performance relationship

over an 11-year period on 30 finishing lines in US steel plants. By focusing on one specific process, and using detailed monthly data on production and HRM practices, this study was well designed to isolate the impact of human resource management on productivity. The positive effects of 'high-performance' practices come through consistently in the econometric analysis. Moreover, the favourable impact of systems of HRM practices on productivity were greater than the sum of the gains from adopting individual practices.

Human Resource Practices Survey Results[1]

The HRPS asked respondents about performance trends in their establishment over the five-year period 1988-93. Three sets of performance indicators were included: those pertaining directly to *labour* (voluntary quits, layoffs, accidents/injuries, and formal grievances/complaints); *efficiency* outcomes (labour productivity, unit costs, customer complaints, and service/product quality); and *financial* outcomes (sales, market share, and profits).

Methodology

Our examination of the relationship between HRM approach and firm performance involved comparing these outcome trends across the three HRM clusters introduced in Chapter 3 – the traditional, compensation-based, and participation-based clusters.

Before turning to the results, the relative strengths and weaknesses of the data should be noted. The HRPS includes data on a wide range of human-resource practices, which has enabled us to characterize establishments on the basis of their overall HRM systems. While the database is relatively strong in measuring the HRM side of the equation, it likely raises more concerns in terms of the performance indicators. On the positive side, information was reported on a number of different measures. However, the measures themselves are based on managers' indications of whether performance had improved or not over the preceding five years. Although there are benefits to this approach,[2] these data are general approximations of performance trends rather than statistics. Finally, the survey sample deserves mention. In particular, the coverage of four sectors offers some control for unobserved influences, but naturally raises questions about whether the results can be generalized to other industries.

Descriptive Findings

Table 16 presents the descriptive results of performance trends by summarizing the percentage of establishments reporting improvements in each of the four measures between 1988 and 1993. Looking first at the labour performance trends (Panel A), for all measures the participation-based cluster had the highest incidence of improvements while the traditional cluster had the lowest. The differences between the three groups meet conventional standards of statistical significance only with respect to quits. Nevertheless, the consistency of the ranking across all four labour-performance measures carries some weight.

There was a statistically significant association between HRM approach and one efficiency outcome, unit costs; here as well the percentage of establishments reporting improvements was lower in the traditional cluster than in either of the other two (Panel B). The same ordering applied to labour-productivity trends; however, the differences fell short of standard significance levels. In the case of the three financial outcomes, there was little difference between the three HRM groups (Panel C).

Table 16

Proportion of Establishments Reporting Improvements in Performance Outcomes, by HRM Cluster, 1988-93

| | HRM cluster | | | |
Performance outcome	Traditional	Compensation	Participation	All
	(Percent)			
A Labour outcomes[1]				
Quits***	42.0	54.0	55.0	48.0
Layoffs	13.0	14.0	19.0	15.0
Accidents	37.0	39.0	46.0	39.0
Grievances	33.0	38.0	40.0	35.0
B Efficiency outcomes				
Labour productivity	79.0	88.0	85.0	82.0
Unit costs **	35.0	49.0	49.0	41.0
Customer complaints[1]	67.0	68.0	72.0	69.0
Product/service quality	95.0	94.0	94.0	95.0
C Financial outcomes				
Sales	63.0	61.0	66.0	63.0
Market share	66.0	72.0	71.0	68.0
Profits	47.0	46.0	52.0	48.0

Source: Estimates by the authors, based on data from the Human Resource Practices Survey.

[1] Improvements are signified by decreases.
**Differences among the groups is significant at the .05 levels.
***Differences among the groups is significant at the .01 levels.

These results illustrate the point that the impact of HRM is most identifiable for performance dimensions that are most influenced by HRM policies. The association with HRM-system choice was strongest for the labour-performance measures, which are meant to be directly influenced by HRM. Among the other performance measures, an association was found for unit costs, which is an important indicator of internal efficiency and as such is more proximate to human-resource effects than financial-performance measures.

If HRM does influence indicators such as sales, market share, and profits, it will be indirectly, through its effect on the labour and efficiency outcomes. At the same time, these financial measures are influenced by a host of other factors unrelated to HRM. In order to control for these other influences, we will now turn to regression analysis. However, it should be noted that the range of potential determinants of financial performance extends beyond the scope of the HRPS database.

Regression Analysis

We have modelled each of the performance trends as a function of the establishment's HRM-system choice as well as a set of control variables. Since the dependent variable is based on whether the establishment reported improved performance or not over the five-year period (1988-93), we have specified the models in the form of logistic regressions that estimate the probability of an establishment reporting improved performance.

Table 17 summarizes the results of the regression analysis of the impact of the HRM system on the 11 establishment performance trends. The models were specified to compare the effects of the compensation- and participation-based systems relative to the traditional model. The complete regression tables, including all of the independent variables, are shown in Appendices C4 and C5.

Rather than showing the regression coefficients themselves in Table 17, we have transformed them into 'elasticities' that measure the impact of HRM-system choice on the probability of an establishment reporting improved performance.[3] The table includes quantitative estimates of the impact only where the corresponding regression coefficient for the HRM variable was significant at the .10 level or better. Where this level of significance was not attained, only the direction of the estimated impact is shown.

Table 17

The Estimated Impact of Choice of HRM Cluster on the Probability of Reporting Improved Performance (Relative to the Traditional Model)[1]

Performance outcome	HRM cluster	
	Compensation	Participation
	(Percent)	
A Labour outcomes[2]		
Quits	10.0	11.0
Layoffs	+	7.0
Accidents	+	11.0
Grievances	+	+
B Efficiency outcomes		
Labour productivity	+	+
Unit costs[2]	20.0	19.0
Customer complaints[2]	+	+
Product/service quality	−	−
C Financial outcomes		
Sales	−	+
Market share	+	+
Profits	−	+

Source: Estimates by the authors, based on data from the Human Resource Practices Survey.

[1] Quantitative impacts are shown only where the regression coefficient is significant at the .10 level or better. Where significance does not reach this level, only the direction of the estimated coefficient is indicated
[2] Improvements are signified by decreases.

The estimated impact of HRM-system choice on the labour performance trends is presented in Panel A. The overall conclusion is that the traditional model has performed relatively poorly, particularly in comparison with the participation-based approach. The regressions point to the positive and statistically significant impact of the participation-based approach on three of the four labour performance measures; that is, an organization with that HRM system had approximately a 10 percent higher probability of having experienced improved quit, layoff, and accident trends than firms with the same organizational characteristics but operating under a traditional HRM approach. A similarly positive relative impact was found for the compensation-based model in the case of quits.

Panel B summarizes the results of the regressions on the efficiency outcomes. The impact of the HRM system variables was statistically significant only in the case of unit costs, where establishments   fol-

proximately 20 percent higher probability of reporting improved performance than those following traditional approaches. While the results for the other three efficiency measures are not statistically significant, it should be noted that the unit-cost trends are based on higher quality data.[4] As a result, it seems reasonable to put some additional weight on these results in evaluating the overall impact on efficiency of the different HRM models.

Turning to the financial-outcome models, the HRM system variables had no significant impact. The factors that were consistently important in explaining these trends were sector, size, region, and especially market conditions (Appendix C5).

Assessing the HRPS Results

In sum, our analysis of the HRPS data reveals that firms that are operating under a traditional HRM model have experienced outcome trends that are poorer than, or at best similar to, those of their counterparts that are operating under more strategic and active compensation– or participation-based models. These differences were most consistently observed for labour-related outcome trends where the participation-based model had an especially favourable impact; there were also significant differences in the case of one important efficiency measure: unit costs. Finally, the analysis offers no evidence of a differential HRM impact on financial performance.

Atlantic Canada Survey Results

In a study prepared for the Human Resource Management Project, Wagar (1994) analyzed the relationships between HRM approach and firm performance, based on data collected in 1993 from 1,277 organizations in the Atlantic provinces. The sample consisted of organizations with at least 20 employees from all sectors.

Methodology

The performance data gathered by Wagar cover 13 different dimensions. For each, managers were asked to assess (on a six-point scale) their organization's current performance and performance trends over the past five years. On the basis of factor analysis, these 13 items were grouped into three performance measures: employee satisfaction, employer-employee relations, and economic performance.[5]

Wagar's analysis of the determinants of these measures of organizational performance involved modelling the establishments' factor scores as a function of three types of HRM practices, two 'corporate ideology' variables, and a set of control variables covering environmental conditions and organizational characteristics.

The HRM variables include the number of HR programs (from a list of 11) reported by the respondent, the number of team-based programs (from a list of five), and whether or not the organization had an incentive-pay program.[6] The two corporate ideology variables are 'progressive decision-making,' which is primarily concerned with the extent to which decision-making and communications are shared throughout the organization, and 'social responsibility,' which is an indicator of the organization's involvement in issues of concern to society.

HRM Links to Firm Performance

The impact of these variables on organizational performance is summarized in Table 18. For each of the three performance factors, the results for current performance and for trends over the past five years are included. As well, we report on two variations of each model: first with the three HRM variables and two corporate ideology variables, and then without the corporate ideology variables. Since the intent in Table 18 is to provide an overview of the conclusions of this analysis, only the signs and levels of significance for these variables are included. (For the full regression results, see Wagar (1994).)

The complete models (marked with a 'C' in Table 18) provide modest evidence that team-based programs positively affect employee satisfaction and that HR programs improve employer-employee relations. However, similar to the HRPS analysis, there were no significant HRM determinants of economic performance (which included both efficiency and financial measures in Wagar's study).

The dominant result from the estimates of the complete models is the strong influence of the corporate ideology measures, especially progressive decision-making. In every iteration, including those where economic performance is the dependent variable, progressive decision-making has a positive and highly significant coefficient.

The alternative model specifications reported in Table 18 (in columns marked 'A') offer another perspective. In these regressions, the ideology variables are omitted. Two things happen as a result. On the

Table 18

Regression Results of the Impact of Selected HRM Practices on Firm Performance, Atlantic Provinces, 1993[1]

Dependent variable	Employee satisfaction				Employer-employee relations				Economic performance			
	Current		Trend[2]		Current		Trend[2]		Current		Trend[2]	
	(C)[3]	(A)[3]	(C)[3]	(A)[3]	(C)[3]	(A)[3]	(C)[3]	(A)[3]	(C)[3]	(A)[3]	(C)[3]	(A)[3]
HR programs	0	+++	0	+++	---	---	---	---	0	+	0	+
Team-based programs	+	+++	++	+++	0	0	0	0	0	+	0	+
Incentive-pay programs	0	0	0	0	-	0	0	0	0	0	0	0
Progressive decision-making	+++	na	+++	na	---	na	---	na	+++	na	+++	na
Social responsibility	+++	na	+++	na	0	na	0	na	+++	na	0	na
R-square	.27	.12	.19	.11	.11	.07	.11	.08	.14	.09	.17	.13
Number of observations	1,118	1,168	1,081	1,122	1,108	1,157	1,066	1,109	991	1,027	973	1,076

Source: Based on Wagar (1994), Atlantic Canada Survey.

[1] Dependent variables are factor scores derived from factor analysis of 13 performance measures. The HR programs and team-based programs variables are specified as the number of programs reported by the respondent. The incentive-pay program variable is a binary variable indicating whether firm has some plan or not. The progressive decision-making and social responsibility variables are calculated according to responses to sets of statements. Control variables include market conditions, technology, union status, employment level and trend, and sector. +++ (---), ++ (--), and + (-) indicate that the regression coefficient is positive (negative) and significant at the .01, .05 or .10 levels, respectively; 0 indicates that the coefficient is insignificant, while na indicates that the variable was not included in the model specification.

[2] Over the past five years.

[3] Two model specifications are reported here. The first, marked 'C' for 'complete' includes the three HRM variables and two corporate ideology variables. The second, marked 'A' for 'alternate' includes the three HRM variables, but not the two corporate ideology variables.

one hand, the HRM variables – specifically, HR programs and team-based programs – become much more important determinants of all the performance measures. This change is most notable with respect to economic performance, where the coefficients for these variables are now positive and statistically significant. On the other hand, without the ideology variables, the explanatory power of each model (indicated by the R-square statistic) diminishes.

What these results indicate is that the ideology variables clearly matter more than HR programs, team-based programs, or incentive-pay plans. The progressive decision-making and social-responsibility measures are indicators of something intangible – commitment to a participative and sharing organizational culture. Wagar's results can be interpreted as evidence that innovative practices and programs on their own are not enough to substantially improve performance. What seems more important is that they be introduced into a supportive work environment.

Summary

In reshaping the Canadian workplace, the crucial question is 'what works'? Our analysis of the links between HRM and firm performance leads to the conclusion that, on balance, the traditional models do not fare as well as the more strategic and active approaches we have considered. This is particularly evident in the case of performance indicators that are directly influenced by human-resource policies. Links to financial outcomes – more remote and influenced by a number of non-HRM factors – are more difficult to identify. Ultimately, a critical point to consider is that the underlying degree of trust and commitment probably means more than the concrete practices alone.

Notes

[1] This discussion is based on Leckie and Betcherman (1994).

[2] The primary advantages of this approach to measuring performance (compared with eliciting more precise quantitative figures) are that it offers the possibility of comparing results across very different organizations and that it encourages organizations to respond to potentially sensitive questions. According to Cooke (1990), informed managers are generally able to assess performance trends relatively accurately.

[3] These elasticities have been calculated at the mean value of the dependent variable. For more details on the methodology, see Leckie and Betcherman (1994).

[4] Respondents were asked whether their organization formally estimated each of these performance measures. The proportions reporting that they did were 66 percent for unit costs, 57 percent for productivity, 46 percent for quality, and 34 percent for complaints.

[5] The satisfaction factor includes morale, organizational commitment, satisfaction with the organization, and quality of life. Employer-employee relations incorporates grievances, absenteeism, turnover, resistance to change, and conflict. Economic performance includes productivity, quality customer/client satisfaction, and profitablility.

[6] The HR programs were formal appraisals, employee-attitude surveys, business-information sharing, pension plan, employee assistance plan, orientation, sexual-harassment policy, grievance procedure for nonunionized employees, job sharing, job enlargement, and an HRM/IR department. The team-based programs were quality circles, quality-of-working life, problem-solving groups, autonomous work teams, and joint employee-management programs. The incentive-pay plans were profit-sharing, productivity gainsharing, and group/team incentives.

5

The Implications of HRM Trends For Workers

In considering the consequences of HRM trends for workers and their unions, we should emphasize two points at the outset. First, as we have seen, most Canadian workplaces do not fit the 'high-performance' model. Second, the implications of HRM trends for workers do not fall neatly into one category, either 'good' or 'bad.' In high-performance, high-commitment workplaces, employees are given a lot of training and support in balancing work and family pressures, and strong firm performance tends to provide some job security. The down side is that wage polarization and concerns about stress and health are increasing, partly as a result of the changing contract between workers and employers.

In this chapter we examine the impact of HRM trends on job security, access to training, balancing work and family, the distribution of wages, stress levels, and health. Then we consider how unions are being affected by developments in human resource management.

Job Security

Job security has become a serious concern for Canadian workers. The recession and major structural changes in the economy have been important underlying factors. In vulnerable industries where shut-downs and large-scale rationalization have become commonplace, job security is now a distant memory.

The difficult economic times, however, cannot fully explain the instability we observe. Another part of the story is that most employers in this country are taking a 'low-commitment' approach to HRM. Our research indicates that the dominant competitive strategies are based on cost-cutting and the adoption of new technologies rather than on the contribution of human resources; only a minority of firms have implemented HR models predicated on a high level of investment in the workforce.

International Comparisons of Job Stability

One manifestation of the low-commitment approach is that Canadian jobs are of relatively short tenure. The high turnover and low stability that characterizes employment in this country is revealed in an international comparison recently made by the OECD (1993). In 1991, almost one-quarter (23.5 percent) of the employed labour force in Canada had been with their current employer for less than one year; the corresponding figures for Japan and Germany were just 9.8 percent and 12.8 percent, respectively. At the other end of the spectrum, 44.6 percent of employed Canadians had been with their employer for five years or more, compared with 59 percent in Germany and 62.6 percent in Japan.

Using job-tenure statistics, the OECD was able to place different countries on an 'employment stability continuum' (Figure 19). The upper-right quadrant, housing those countries where employment is least stable, includes Canada.

That these variations cannot be explained by workforce differences such as age or sex composition suggests that the important variables are institutional ones, including those affecting the relationship and the level of commitment between employees and employers. Indeed, as we saw in Chapter 4, there is a statistically significant relationship between turnover and HRM approach in which the traditional cluster does not fare as well as the compensation-based or participation-based groups.

It should be noted that some degree of flexibility in the labour market is desirable – it is necessary to match people and jobs effectively and it allows structural change to occur efficiently and with a minimum amount of dislocation. However, a labour market with a very high turnover rate and low-tenure jobs could create too much instability for workers and lead to personal hardship and insecurity

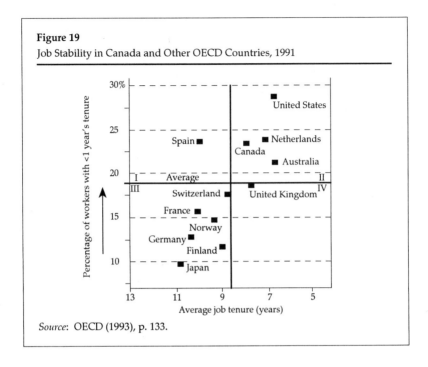

Figure 19
Job Stability in Canada and Other OECD Countries, 1991

Source: OECD (1993), p. 133.

about the future. It could also limit the degree of employee commitment to the workplace.

Too much turnover and not enough stability may well constrain the development of skills as well. The OECD found that countries characterized by relatively low-tenure jobs tend to be those with the least workplace training. In addition to not having a lot of *job* security, Canadian workers often do not have the opportunity to enhance their general *employment* security (i.e., their ability to find another job) by upgrading their skills in their current job.

Nonstandard Employment

Another dimension of job security concerns the types of jobs being created, and in particular the proliferation of nonstandard employment such as part-time, short-term, and temporary work. These jobs are virtually by definition less secure, in terms of both employment and income security, than full-time, long-term positions.

In Chapter 3, we reported results from the Human Resource Practices Survey (HRPS) showing that employers were increasing their use of part-time, short-term, and contract workers. National statistics also show a significant upward trend over time in the incidence of nonstandard employment (Figure 20). In 1993, close to 30 percent of all jobs fit into one of the nonstandard categories. Further, nonstandard work has accounted for much of the net increase in total employment since 1980.

Employer preference is a key factor explaining the growth in nonstandard employment. According to the HRPS, firms use nonstandard employment because it offers flexibility, and to a lesser extent, cost savings. One indicator of the increasing employer preference for nonstandard work forms is the growth in involuntary part-time employment, defined as part-time jobs filled by workers who would prefer full-time jobs. The proportion of involuntary part-time employment has been growing, reaching 35.5 percent in 1993, the highest share on record (Figure 21).

While current economic conditions are linked to growing job insecurity, then, that insecurity is also a consequence of the low-commitment HRM systems adopted in much of Canadian industry. It is

Figure 20

Nonstandard Employment[1] as a Proportion of Total Employment, Canada, 1975-93

Source: Estimates by the authors, based on data from Statistics Canada.
1 Nonstandard employment as defined here consists of part-time employment, short-tenure (full-time) employment, and independent contracting (full-time, long-term).

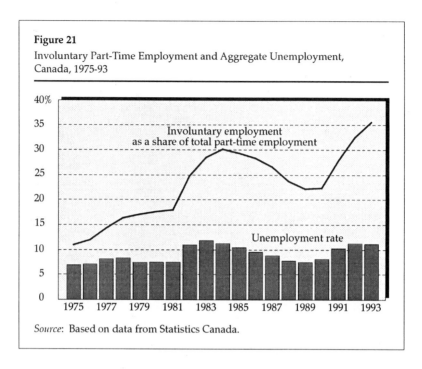

Figure 21

Involuntary Part-Time Employment and Aggregate Unemployment, Canada, 1975-93

Source: Based on data from Statistics Canada.

clearly difficult to make long-term job guarantees in the current economic climate; however, high-performance workplaces can deliver more security because the organizations themselves are more likely to be doing well and have a higher commitment to workers, and their greater investment in training enhances general employability.

Access to Workplace Training

A positive relationship between employees' access to workplace training and job tenure has been well-established in a number of studies (Mincer 1988; OECD 1993). And while the causes of this have been difficult to disentangle, analysis suggests that there is a synergy between employers' investment in employees and workers' loyalty to the firm.

Who Gets Workplace Training?

Only a minority of workers – according to the National Training Survey 36 percent in 1991 – get employer-sponsored training. The average amount of training for *all* workers was 14 hours (Canadian

Labour Market and Productivity Centre 1993). The results of the Adult Education and Training Survey, which collected information from individuals (rather than organizations), were very similar: among full-time employees with at least one year's tenure in their current jobs, 30 percent participated in some employer-sponsored training in 1991. The average across all workers was 20 hours of training (Kapsalis 1993).

The distribution of enterprise-based training is also very uneven. Employers tend to concentrate their investment on prime-aged workers and on employees who already have a high level of human capital. According to the Adult Education and Training Survey, for example, workplace training is most frequently reported by employees between the ages of 25 and 44, after which it begins to fall off significantly (Table 19). And among full-time employees who have at least one year's job tenure, university graduates and those who earn at least $35,000 are more than three times as likely to receive employer-sponsored training as those without postsecondary education or who earn less than $20,000.

The low level and relatively poor distribution of employer-sponsored training is consistent with the low-commitment HRM models

Table 19

Incidence of Employer-Based Training Among Full-Time Workers with at Least One Year's Tenure, by Selected Employee Characteristics, Canada, 1991.

Employee characteristics	Employees participating in employer-based training
	(Percent)
Age (years)	
17-24	26.0
25-34	33.0
35-44	34.0
45-54	27.0
55-64	17.0
Education level	
0-8 years	6.0
Some secondary	14.0
High school	28.0
Some postsecondary	36.0
Postsecondary diploma	34.9
University degree	44.0
Annual earnings	
Under $20,000	15.0
$20,000 - $34,999	29.0
$35,000+	46.0

Source: Kapsalis (1993, 10), Adult Education and Training Survey.

that predominate in Canadian industry today. In high-performance workplaces, employers recognize that in order to deliver results, especially in an environment of rapid change, employees need the tools to be multi-skilled, flexible, and responsible. For that they need training.

Balancing Work and Family

In Chapter 3, we discussed the relatively low incidence of HRM practices designed to help workers deal with the pressures of balancing work and family obligations. However, the bottom line is that such pressure translates into costs – most obviously to employees and their families, but also to employers.

Stresses from Balancing Work and Family

Respondents to the HRPS were asked whether work-family conflict manifested itself in workplace problems. Close to two-thirds reported that it did. The impact of work-family conflict most often takes the form of absenteeism, tardiness, and employees demanding alternative scheduling arrangements (Table 20).

In their study of work and family, Higgins, Duxbury, and Lee (1992) collected data on a range of employee outcomes.[1] With respect to work-family conflict, and specifically 'role overload,' not surprisingly levels were greatest among women with children at home. High degrees of stress were reported by over one-half of the women surveyed, especially mothers in dual-'earner' families and by single parents.[2]

The evidence of the negative impact of balancing work and family stands in sharp relief with the HRPS results (reported in Chapter 3) showing that relatively few firms (and employees) have flexible working arrangements or family-care benefits.

Part-Time Arrangements as a Balancing Tool

HRM practices such as flexible scheduling and family-care benefits are one way to reduce the conflict employees experience in dealing with work and family responsibilities. Research by Duxbury and Higgins (1994) for the Human Resource Management Project indicates that part-time employment can also be a way for some workers, especially working mothers, to deal with the stress arising from balancing work and family. While the benefits of part-time work varied for different

Table 20

Proportion of Establishments Reporting Increases in Selected Indicators due to Work and Family Pressures on Employees, by Sector, 1993

Indicator	Wood products	Fabricated metal products	Electrical and electronic products	Selected business services	All sectors
			(Percent)		
Absenteeism or tardiness	47.2	57.5	64.3	53.0	55.6
Demand for alternative scheduling arrangements	20.4	22.6	32.2	42.7	29.8
Turnover	12.5	5.4	15.4	16.2	12.1
Difficulty in promoting from within	7.4	5.9	7.7	10.8	8.0
None of the above	41.5	36.6	27.3	33.5	34.6

Source: Estimates by the authors, based on data from the Human Resource Practices Survey.

groups of women surveyed, most reported favourable outcomes. Some of their findings include the following:

- Compared with women who are in full-time 'earner' positions, part-time women earners reported significantly less role over-load, fewer difficulties in managing family time, significantly less stress and depression, and greater satisfaction with life.
- While a major issue associated with part-time work is pay and benefit levels, how much of an issue it is depends on whether the part-time employee is in a career or an earner position. Both groups reported receiving the same (relative) earnings as their full-time counterparts; however, 40 percent of the earner part-timers did not receive pro-rated benefits; this is compared with only 12 percent of career part-timers, who more frequently bar-gain from a position of greater power.
- The majority of part-time employees exhibited a high level of work commitment, work expectations, and job satisfaction, pos-itive outcomes that were related to the fact that they had flexibility and discretion over when they worked.

Despite such evidence of the positive contribution of voluntary nonstandard arrangements like part-time work, many Canadian firms still do not support them. Only 28 percent of the HRPS establishments reported that they had *voluntary* nonstandard workers. Since this is an indicator of commitment to the workforce, it is not surprising that this figure was significantly greater in the participation- and compensation-based HRM clusters (36 and 35 percent, respectively) than in the traditional one (21 percent).

Wages

What role do HRM strategies play in the stagnation of wages and growing inequality of earnings in the Canadian labour market? On the one hand, choices firms are making regarding compensation cannot be viewed as the major factor in the *stagnation* of wage levels – the HRPS data as well as the interviews conducted by Downie and Coates (1994) emphasize the competitive pressures and constraints facing all employers on the labour-cost front. On the other hand, HRM practices may well be playing some role in the changing *distribution* of wages.

HRM and Wage Differentials

The Working With Technology Survey (WWTS) data show that wage disparities grew between 1985 and 1991. Using various measures, the WWTS data indicate that, within establishments, wage differentials between high- and low-paid occupational groups increased by 5 to 8 percent.[3]

HRM practices seem to be contributing to these disparities in at least two ways. The first is the fact that access to employer-sponsored training is positively associated with earnings levels: already relatively well paid workers receive a disproportionate share of the overall investment while lower paid employees receive relatively little. Given the established link between workplace training and subsequent wage gains, this can be expected to increase overall wage differentials.[4]

The second factor is the diffusion of certain nontraditional HRM practices, most notably variable pay. The 1991 WWTS data were used to compare occupational wage differentials in establishments with different HRM practices (Table 21). The results indicate that these differentials were lowest in organizations operating with traditional

Table 21

Occupational Wage Differentials[1] and Human-Resource Practices, 1991.

Human-resource practice	Managers and other office workers	Professional and technical and other office workers	Skilled and unskilled	Highest and lowest
	A. Between-occupation wage differentials			
Neither employee participation nor variable pay	2.36	1.46	1.37	4.12
Variable pay only	2.67	1.72	1.39	5.03
Both employee participation and variable pay	2.73	1.77	1.48	5.23
	B. Within-occupation wage differentials			
Neither employee participation nor variable pay	1.79	1.75	1.48	
Variable pay only	2.17	2.10	1.75	
Both employee participation and variable pay	2.10	1.53	1.77	

Source: Estimates by the authors, based on data from the Working With Technology Survey.

[1] Mean ratio of mean weekly wages and salaries of the highest-paid to the lowest-paid full-time employees.

models (defined as having neither employee- participation nor variable-pay programs). Where establishments had introduced variable-pay plans, wage differentials were significantly higher. These results apply both to between-occupation and within-occupation differentials.

This analysis suggests, then, that wage dispersions widen when compensation is linked to contribution or performance. This finding is not surprising given that variable-pay plans are often explicitly designed to break the standardizing and centralizing tendencies associated with traditional wage-setting policies.

Many of these wage differentials widen further in establishments that have adopted both variable pay and formal employee-participation programs. Why this is so is not clear from the survey data; perhaps establishments with both types of practices have moved away from traditional wage policies more definitively than establishments with variable pay alone.

Thus, while the high-performance workplace model has many positive attributes, it also may have a down side in that it generates more polarized wage structures.[5] At the societal level, of course, growing earnings inequalities create a number of pressures relating to the adequacy of earnings and equity.

Stress and Health

From the perspective of employees, problems with health and stress are among the most important in workplace reorganization, and more broadly, changing expectations regarding work.

The United Steelworkers of America Workplace Reorganization Survey (WRS), conducted for the Human Resource Management Project, collected information from presidents of USWA locals in Ontario on workplace reorganization in their bargaining units (Ekos Research Associates 1993b).[6] The officers were asked whether new job designs, new work systems, new pay systems, or new training systems had been introduced into their workplaces over the preceding five years. Where at least one of these changes had taken place, they were asked their reactions to a series of statements about how the workplace reorganization had affected various aspects of their members' work.

The results are summarized in Table 22. The survey asked about a range of issues including job security, training, control over work, and

Table 22

Impact of Workplace Reorganization between 1988 and 1993 on Union Members,[1] According to Union Local Presidents, Ontario

Impact	Agree	Neutral	Disagree
		(Percent)	
Job security has increased	22.0	43.0	35.0
Skill requirements have increased	47.0	40.0	13.0
Input into decisions has decreased	26.0	45.0	29.0
Training and promotion opportunities have increased	21.0	41.0	38.0
Wages and benefits have increased	41.0	41.0	18.0
Health and safety concerns have increased	54.0	33.0	13.0
Job stress has decreased	13.0	49.0	39.0
Contact with fellow workers has decreased	15.0	46.0	39.0

Source: Ekos Research Associates Inc. (1993b), Workplace Reorganization Survey.

[1] Responses were on a seven-point scale. The top two points indicate agreement, the middle three indicate a neutral position, and the bottom two indicate disagreement.

wages, but none elicited as strong a response as health and safety. Over half the local presidents agreed that workplace reorganization had increased their members' concerns with health and safety; only 13 percent disagreed with this statement. The WRS data also suggest that workplace reorganization can be stressful; 39 percent of the respondents disagreed with the statement that job stress had decreased while just 13 percent agreed with it.[7]

These results are consistent with qualitative evidence that some nontraditional workplace practices, including tying pay to performance, shifting responsibility onto the line, and moving to job enlargement and rotation, can exact a price on employees. These negative effects of nontraditional workplace practices, concerns about job security (especially among 'survivors' of downsizing measures), and a preoccupation with productivity growth, efficiency, and competitiveness, have led many employers to 'speed up' their operations and put pressure on employees to work longer and harder.

Obviously, how new workplace practices are put in place can be important. In fact, the WRS data indicate that where the union has been involved in the planning and implementation process, the impact of the reorganization on the workforce tends to be more favourably perceived.[8]

HRM Trends and Unions

What do changing HRM patterns mean for labour unions? Under the traditional approaches, acceptable tradeoffs between labour and management had evolved over time. These tradeoffs offered guarantees not only for workers, but also for unions as the exclusive vehicle for worker representation.

As we saw in Chapter 2, employers' initiatives to introduce nontraditional HRM systems pose a dilemma for organized labour. Practices involving teamwork, incentive pay, and the sharing of information and decision-making are designed to align the interests of workers and employers, link rewards to performance, and reinforce direct communication between individual workers and management. While many goals may be served by such policies, they can, either intentionally or unintentionally, break down the principles that underlie the role of the union and collective bargaining in the workplace: the fundamentally different interests of labour and management, the inherent power imbalance between the two, and the need for independent worker representation.

There is no doubt that the impact of workplace innovation on organized labour has not always been positive. In addition to the ideological difficulties, unions often have identified the risk, insecurity, and increased workload that can accompany reorganization. And it should not be forgotten that workplace change in recent years has often been accompanied by downsizing and insecurity. Consequently, unions have frequently resisted it to the extent that was feasible. More recently, as discussed in Chapter 2, some unions have started to accept the inevitability of restructuring and have begun developing more proactive strategies.

Interviews with Union Leaders

Our interviews with union leaders support many of these points (Downie and Coates 1994; Kumar 1994). Labour leaders acknowledge the possibility that new workplace initiatives will be used to drive a wedge between workers and their union. However, they generally believe that the key for unions is to ensure that they still have something to offer workers. Workplace reorganization can be either a threat or an opportunity for the union; as one leader put it:

> '[I]f the local union does not do anything ... does not try to develop an agenda on trying to improve the workplace on behalf of workers, then yes it runs the risk of being carved out of the picture and being painted a third party and being distanced from the workers. On the other hand, if a local union can rise to the occasion, bring its own agenda to the discussions on workplace change ... and basically tries to improve the nature of work in the workplace, it will really strengthen the union.' (Downie and Coates 1994)

The interviews suggest that employers and unions are increasingly discussing workplace reorganization. In this sense labour is being brought into, or moving into, nontraditional areas. Many unions seem to be playing a more active role in the workplace, and there is an increasing number of joint labour-management initiatives in training and other aspects of work reorganization.

However, union leaders believe that labour's participation is often sought only after the employer's agenda has been set. Overall, our research did not find much evidence of real cooperation or 'strategic alliances' between the parties to reshape the organization of the workplace.

The Impact of Workplace Reorganization on Union Locals

To this point, much of the debate over workplace reorganization has taken place in the national and district headquarters of various labour unions. Very little information has been collected at the workplace level about the impact of HRM changes on unions as institutions. One of the objectives of the USWA Workplace Reorganization Survey was to investigate the local officials' perspectives on the impact of changing practices on their union.

The WRS also questioned local presidents about the impact of workplace reorganization on their local over the past five years (Table 23). Where changes had taken place, officials were asked their reactions to seven statements about how their union local had been affected. They were questioned on the impact on union involvement in the workplace, members' attitudes towards the union, union decision-making, and relations with management. The responses suggest that the impact of workplace reorganization on locals has not been dra-

Table 23

Impact of Workplace Reorganization between 1988 and 1993 on Union Locals[1] According to Union Local Presidents, Ontario

Impact	Agree	Neutral	Disagree
		(Percent)	
More union involvement	31.0	41.0	28.0
More militant membership	19.0	43.0	37.0
Less loyal and committed members	23.0	50.0	27.0
Change in the work of local offices	39.0	44.0	17.0
More member input into union decisions	37.0	52.0	11.0
Local officers too close to management	5.0	35.0	60.0
Job stress has decreased	13.0	43.0	44.0

Source: Ekos Research Associates Inc. (1993b), from the Workplace Reorganization Survey, 1993.

[1] Responses were on a seven-point scale. The top two points indicate agreement, the middle three indicate neutral position, and the bottom two indicate disagreement.

matic (Ekos Research Associates 1993b). Most often the effects were reported as neutral.

On the subject of the impact of workplace reorganization on the attitudes of members, more officials disagreed than agreed with the statement that it had made them more militant. As these HRM changes typically have been intended to strengthen workers' identification with the firm, this is not unexpected. However, there is also little evidence of members becoming less loyal or committed to the union.

The responses suggest that the operation of the local frequently changed where workplaces had been reorganized. A significant number of presidents agreed that the work of local officers had changed, and that the membership now had more input into union decision-making.

One possible concern for unions in workplace reorganization is whether they can remain independent. Presidents were asked whether they felt that, with workplace reorganization, officers were getting too close to management and whether the membership perceived this to be the case. Few thought this was happening – only 5 percent – and just 13 percent believed their members thought this was happening.

Summary

Trends in human resource management have significant consequences for workers. Short job tenure, high turnover, and the increase in employer-driven nonstandard employment have created an unstable environment. This instability is but one manifestation of the low commitment to employees on the part of most employers today. Another is the low level and biased distribution of workplace training. Current HRM practices also are inadequate in addressing employees' work-family conflicts. A high level of commitment could do much to enable workers to manage the pressures of today's workplace, with positive outcomes for overall performance.

Nevertheless, it is also clear that the high-performance model – at least as it tends to be implemented – could have some negative consequences. Two we have identified are the association between these systems and wage polarization, and declining health and increased stress. The long-run viability of this model will be determined in part by how well these issues are addressed.

Notes

[1] The work and family database used for this study and the study by Duxbury and Higgins (1994) for the Human Resource Management Project is briefly described in Chapter 3.

[2] Duxbury and Higgins classify workers into two categories: 'earners' (clerical, administrative, technical, retail, and production occupations) and 'career' employees (managerial and professional occupations).

[3] Using mean establishment weekly wages and salaries of full-time employees, we measured occupational wage differentials in three ways: (1) the ratio of management to 'other office' (clerical) salaries; (2) the ratio of professional/technical to 'other office' salaries; and (3) the ratio of skilled production to general unskilled wages. These ratios increased between 1985 and 1991 by 5.8, 6.5, and 7.8 percent, respectively.

[4] For a review of the relevant literature, see Betcherman (1993).

[5] It should be pointed out that other forces, such as technological change, may be at play here as well. Among WWTS respondents, wage dispersion was positively correlated with the degree to which computer-based technologies had been introduced (Caron 1993). Since CBT use was also correlated with the adoption of nontraditional HRM practices such as variable pay and employee involvement, it is difficult to disentangle the precise relationships.

[6] These bargaining units were predominantly in manufacturing workplaces. For more detail on the Workplace Reorganization Survey, see Appendix B.

[7] We interpret these results to be primarily indicators that workplace reorganization often brings with it health problems and increased stress. However, the WRS data could also be interpreted as evidence that reorganization does not lead to these problems as much as it heightens the employees' awareness of the impact on health and stress of the design and operation of their workplace.

[8] One mechanism for union involvement is a labour-management agreement on workplace reorganization. Thirty percent of the USWA locals surveyed reported that such an agreement had been negotiated. On most dimensions, including job security, skill and training, wages, and control over work, the impace of workplace reorganization on members was judged by officials to be more favourable where agreements were in place (Ekos Research Associates 1993b).

6

A High-Performance Workplace Model for Canada

In summarizing the major findings of our research, our starting point is that traditional human resource management systems are no longer effectively meeting the goals of management, workers, or Canadian society. From this position we will sketch the essential elements of a high-performance workplace model that fits with the new economic, social, and technological environment. In many respects, this model runs counter to longstanding attitudes and institutions, and as a result its diffusion will require a concerted effort by industry, labour, and government.

What Have We Learned?

Our research has led us to conclude that this is a critical period for human resource management in Canada. Major changes in the environment are forcing business and labour to rethink the traditional approaches. While some are experimenting with alternative HRM systems for the 'new economy,' there is no consensus on a new Canadian model. In effect, we are now at a crossroads.

A Changing Environment

There is no doubt that Canadian business is facing a rapidly shifting, and often difficult, environment. The major changes include the following:

- *Increasing competition* is forcing firms to search for continuous improvements in productivity and quality and greater flexibility to respond to market demands;
- *Technological change* is creating new skills and eliminating old ones, breaking down traditional organizational hierarchies, and rerouting the flow of information and decision-making;
- *The labour force is changing* – it is better educated, more diverse, and has very different needs and expectations than previous workforces; and
- *New regulatory requirements* have made compliance and policy-setting in the HRM area more complex for most firms.

HRM Priority? More Rhetoric than Reality

As a result of these developments, virtually all organizations have had to reconsider all their strategies and practices, from how they position themselves in the marketplace to how they approach human resource management.

It is now conventional wisdom that human resources must be *the* priority; they are the key to success in an increasingly competitive, high-technology environment. Companies routinely assert that people and their skills – and, by extension, HRM – are critical to their operations. We have found that in reality this is often not the case.

Two lines of evidence support this contention. The first is data on business strategies that suggest that in fact Canadian firms more often base their competitive strategies on cutting costs and introducing new technology. Strategic approaches that place human resources front and centre are less typical and often at odds with the dominant strategies.

The second and more direct body of evidence comes from our analysis of HRM practices. The majority of firms we studied still operate under traditional models that place a low priority on human resources and are based on a low level of commitment between employer and worker. These organizations tend not to integrate HR issues into overall business plans, have Taylorist job designs and work processes, have a low level of investment in training, rarely share information or decision-making with workers or their unions, make limited use of compensation to create positive incentives, and do not have family-care programs.

The Limits to Traditional HRM Models

Low-priority, low-commitment HRM models were adequate when markets were expanding consistently, technological change involved incremental improvements to exploit economies of scale, the labour force consisted predominantly of high-school educated males, and regulatory requirements were straightforward. Now that the environment has been turned on its head, the old systems are proving to be limited.

Several problems are emerging as a result of the continued predominance of these HRM models, including concerns that equity and efficiency are being compromised. This affects the welfare of workers, the performance of firms, the efficiency of the labour market, and the rate of economic growth.

A High Degree of Employment Insecurity

We are living in very insecure times. For many workers, the insecurity associated with the weak economy and structural and technological change is aggravated because employers are not offering them much long-term commitment.

The Canadian labour market is characterized by high turnover, short job tenure, and a high proportion of part-time, short-term, and other forms of 'nonstandard' workers. This is in contrast with some other countries that have a higher level of commitment. While there are some advantages to this lower commitment in the form of economic efficiency, the accompanying instability has major costs.[1]

While it is unrealistic to expect a return to the economic security of 1945-75, the current level of insecurity is dysfunctional and imposes high personal costs on workers. Low-commitment HRM approaches offer no *job security*, and little in the way of *employment security* – that is, they do not prepare workers for other positions within the firm or enhance their general employability. This can reduce efficiency for firms and for the labour market.

Economic insecurity is also becoming more unequally distributed over time. Well-educated and highly skilled workers are now not immune to insecurity, but they are generally much more able to protect themselves from job loss (or at least income loss) and to exploit new opportunities than their less-skilled counterparts. This disparity will increase as technological change demands even higher levels of skill. HRM practices in Canadian industry contribute to this polarization, because the limited investment in human resources is concentrated on employees who already have greater skills.

Insufficient Human-Resource Development

Human capital has always been a major source of economic growth, and it is virtually certain that its contribution is increasing as the economy becomes more technology- and knowledge-intensive. While many forms of training and education contribute to prosperity, the economic returns are often highest when skills are acquired in the work setting. In the future, accelerating technological change will inevitably lead to skill upgrading while a slowdown in labour-force growth will limit the extent to which these skill requirements can be met by new, highly-educated workers. These trends will further increase the importance of workplace training.

Certainly, ambitious training efforts are now in place in some firms. However, the overall training effort in Canadian workplaces is still not adequate. Too many firms do not invest enough in training and too many workers, especially those with lower levels of human capital, have no access to training opportunities.

A low-priority, low-commitment HRM approach is not compatible with a high level of training for a number of reasons. Most importantly, employers are unlikely to invest in training employees with short job tenure or in contingent, nonstandard positions. As well, where job designs are traditional, or highly 'articulated' (i.e., involving narrow, repetitive tasks), there are few returns to extensive training.

Excessive Reliance on Layoffs

All economies are now experiencing a great deal of adjustment as old industries and occupations die and new ones emerge. For workers, this adjustment can involve some combination of learning new skills, changing jobs, or even relocating. This process can take place within the firm – the 'internal' labour market – or in the 'external' labour market.

How this adjustment occurs depends in part on the firm's HRM strategy. In Europe and Japan there is a high degree of commitment to employees, and much of the adjustment takes place in the internal labour market. In contrast, Canada's low-commitment approach – unstable employment relationships and limited firm investment in employees – creates little incentive for employers to internalize the adjustment process through reassignment, retraining, or redistribution of working hours.

More typically Canadian firms rely on layoffs to respond to changing business conditions. As a result, the adjustment process tends to take place in the 'external' labour market; i.e., unemployed workers search for new jobs or acquire new skills through training programs or in educational institutions.

While many workers manage this adjustment quite smoothly, there are a number of concerns about how effective it really is. These include:

- the high and persistent level of structural and long-term unemployment;
- the substantial cost of unemployment insurance benefits and the high premiums paid by employees and employers to finance them; and
- the ineffectiveness of institutional training (that is, disconnected from the workplace) in leading to employment, particularly stable employment, for dislocated workers.[2]

Stresses Balancing Work and Family Responsibilities

Historically, there has been a sharp separation between the realms of work and home, which was functional as long as the workforce was predominantly male and there was a traditional division of labour within the family. It is becoming less so, however, as women (especially those with young children) increasingly participate in the labour force and as the nature of the family changes. Balancing work and family responsibilities has become an important issue, and it will become more so.[3]

Canadian employers are generally not responding adequately to these new pressures. 'Family-friendly' policies such as flexible scheduling, work-at-home, job-sharing, and family-care benefits are not available to the majority of workers. In the longer run, however, firms that continue to see the job and the home as mutually exclusive realms will pay for it through low productivity and high turnover.

Inferior Firm Performance

This study has reinforced the growing evidence that traditional HRM systems are associated with poor firm performance. Establishments organized along conventional lines typically compare unfavourably with those that make a sustained and coordinated effort to involve employees in decision-making, invest in developing their skills, and use compensation to reward performance.

All other things being equal, then, workplaces where HRM has a low priority and there is low commitment to employees are likely to be low-performance workplaces. This is due to the increasingly poor fit between these systems and the context in which they now must operate. This new environment calls for a degree of operational flexibility, the ability to improve productivity and quality continuously, and a more progressive and challenging work environment than the traditional models can deliver. From a global perspective, these HRM systems no longer offer a workable recipe to create competitive companies or a strong, innovative national economy.

A High-Performance Workplace Model for the New Economy

An effective, high-performance workplace model should incorporate a number of elements. First and foremost, it should be a high-performance model for *all* of the principal stakeholders – business, labour, and society. Second, it must realistically reflect the economic constraints we face now and are likely to continue to face in the foreseeable future. And third, it should be compatible with Canadian institutions, values, and culture (rather than simply be an imported solution).

The Elements of a Workable Model

In recent years, various programs – from quality circles to total quality management – have been touted as *the* means to achieving a high-performance workplace. As each of these has had its day, it has become clear that there are no magic solutions. Commitment and trust are the essential ingredients if programs like these are to succeed. Moreover, piecemeal innovation does not work; organizations need to adopt a coherent, integrated approach to workplace reorganization.

There is no uniform approach to HRM that fits all. The particular characteristics of a high-performance workplace model in a particular firm will depend on characteristics such as its history, culture, size, industry, workforce, and union status. Nevertheless, while the specifics may vary, an effective high-performance workplace model must include the following elements:[4]

- *a flexible work organization* where work rules and job descriptions are fluid, employees are able to use discretion to get the job done, and formal and informal hierarchies are minimized;
- a commitment to *training* to deepen and broaden employees' skills;
- increased *employee involvement and participation* in the operation of the organization;
- policies to promote *sharing*, most obviously of the financial rewards from good performance, but also of information and privilege;
- a *work process designed to improve health and reduce stress*; and
- *family-friendly policies* that support employees in balancing their work and domestic responsibilities.

What are the Tradeoffs?

Workplace reorganization can only be successful if it holds the promise of real benefits for both the employer and the employees. Because their interests are not identical, an effective model must involve acceptable tradeoffs. The tradeoffs associated with the high-performance model are highlighted in Figure 22.

For employers, the attraction is enhanced firm performance and increased competitiveness. Although it is important to cut costs and adopt new technologies, without the six elements of the high-performance workplace described above, these are not enough. The tradeoff for employers also includes higher costs in the short run – placing greater emphasis on attaching a priority to human resource initiatives requires investment. More fundamentally, a high-performance workplace model requires employers to reconsider historical notions about management's prerogative. The degree of employee initiative, involvement, and commitment implied by the model cannot occur without much more sharing of information and decision-making.

Figure 22
The Benefits and Costs of the High-Performance Model

	Benefits	Costs
For firms	Efficiency gains	Greater investment in training and other HR programs
	Lower turnover	Have to share information
	Better employee-employer relations	Have to share decision-making
	Potential for a better bottom line	
For workers	Access to information	No guarantee of job security
	Participation in decision-making	Need for greater commitment to the organization
	Discretion over work process	Some compensation based on performance
	Enhanced employability	
	Support for family responsibilities	
For unions	Affirmation of an independent voice for workers	Can take positions on work organization
	Access to information	Move away from job-control unionism
	Input into range of workplace issues	

For workers, the model offers a great deal. It provides an opportunity for increased access to information, enables them to participate in decision-making, gives them far greater discretion over the work process, and places more emphasis on social and health needs than has been the case under traditional systems. Also, the high-performance workplace strives to be a 'learning organization,' both through formal and informal training. Finally, it supports employment security by enhancing workers' employability. However, the model does not offer a complete job-security pledge, nor does it provide the protection of narrow job definitions and seniority-based deployment. While companies should certainly value long-term attachments, job security can rarely be guaranteed any longer. The model also asks a lot of employees in terms of participating in the organization and accepting that some portion of their compensation will depend on performance.

The reorganized workplace creates both opportunities and threats for labour unions. Certainly, given the strength of unions in this country, the viability of the high-performance model depends on the opportunities outweighing the threats. By emphasizing employee participation, the model is in a sense tailor-made for unions, a major part of whose raison d'être is to represent workers. Indeed, research suggests that an *independent* employee voice is critical to the high-performance workplace.[5] In order for unions to be able to play a major role, there are prerequisites: first, employers must be willing to establish a dialogue with labour on issues that have traditionally been management prerogatives, and second, unions must take a proactive position on workplace reorganization by broadening their agenda and giving up some of the security associated with job-control unionism.

Towards High-Performance Workplaces

Despite their advantages, high-performance workplaces are far from the standard in this country. For example, less than half of the establishments responding to the Human Resource Practices Survey fit into either the compensation– or the participation-based models; and most of those that do have implemented only some of the models' important elements. Moreover, for technical reasons, our data overrepresent their incidence.[6]

Why are high-performance workplaces not more widely diffused in Canada? Four factors seem to be important.

- Much of Canadian business and labour is unaware of the importance of workplace reorganization and high-performance systems, including their critical elements, how they should be implemented, and what the potential benefits can be;
- Immediate economic pressures have made it difficult for firms to take the long-term perspective that would be necessary to commit themselves to a high-performance workplace;
- Many public policies and institutions are not designed to support the high-performance model, and in some cases they even create disincentives to move towards it;
- Fourth, and most fundamentally, workplace reform involves *social* change, which is a very difficult process.

It is possible to overcome these obstacles. But to do so will involve all of the stakeholders, and in some cases it will involve reconsidering old assumptions and attitudes.

Better Information

Information on the model and its impact should be made accessible. While many firms are experiencing the limitations of traditional HRM approaches, most do not have an alternative vision. This is also frequently true of workers, unions, and governments.

The information gap may be most serious for employers, with whom workplace reorganization typically originates. For them, the most compelling motive for adopting new strategies is the promise of improved performance. More research is needed, however, to fully document the links between HRM practices and performance.

It is also important that workers have a better understanding of the implications of different HRM approaches if they and their unions are to make an informed contribution to workplace reorganization. Often labour does not have sufficient access to the necessary expertise to be able do this.

Governments also have a stake in better information; public policy in a range of areas would be enhanced by an understanding of trends in workplace organization. (We will turn to public policy later in this chapter.)

In addition to the diffusion of existing knowledge, new research is required in several areas. These include the following:

- monitoring of workplace practices;
- the impact of different HRM approaches on various aspects of firm performance;
- the links between HRM practices and wages, the incidence of nonstandard employment, access to benefits, and investment in training;
- the environmental factors and strategic choices that facilitate organizational change; and
- the impact of various public policies on HRM practices.

While Canadian analysis in these areas is at the embryonic stage, much more is taking place in other countries, especially the US. Some countries, such as the UK and Australia, have undertaken national workplace surveys and are using them as important inputs into human-resource policies. A similar survey should be undertaken in Canada.

Finally, small firms and labour unions have limited resources, which makes it difficult for them to develop expertise on workplace reorganization. This lack of information makes them wary of moving away from traditional approaches. It is important, then, that governments and umbrella groups for business and labour provide support for research, education, and the dissemination of information.

Growth-Oriented Macroeconomic Policies

Economic theorists are currently rediscovering the contribution that innovation, knowledge, and ideas make to aggregate growth.[7] These are *human* inputs, and as such they are likely to be greatest where work environments are organized to maximize them, i.e., in high-performance workplaces.

It is important to recognize that the diffusion of high performance workplaces is affected by the economic climate. Even where business and labour understand the long-term benefits, economic pressure can make it very difficult for firms to make the necessary investments. In situations dominated by layoffs, shutdowns, and other forms of rationalization, the commitment and trust that provide the fuel for a high-performance approach are unlikely to be present.

When formulating macroeconomic policy, policy-makers should understand that choices at that level have important ramifications for what happens in the workplace. Periods of recession and cutbacks actively discourage the trust and commitment that are essential for workplace innovation and can therefore curtail its contribution to economic growth in the longer run.

Supportive Human Resource Policies and Institutions

One of the themes of our study is the close synergy between organizations and their environment. An important element of that environment is the network of public policies and regulations. These currently do not provide the support or incentives to encourage high-performance workplaces. The following measures would contribute to the reorientation of policies and institutions, a reorientation that is necessary if they are to be more supportive of workplace change.

Support for Workplace Partnerships

Many institutions attempt to work out solutions on the basis of competitive, adversarial relationships. While this type of relationship has a role to play, the new economy requires more cooperation and partnership. In the workplace, laws and institutions have supported a mode of governance based on separable employer and employee interests, reserved management rights, and legalistic procedures for resolving disputes. The result has been the creation of many disincentives and few incentives for employers and workers (with or without a union) to pursue the strategic partnerships that building a high-performance workplace requires.[8]

Such partnerships cannot be legislated. Nevertheless, public policy can encourage them by creating structures and services that support and facilitate them. In recent years, federal and provincial governments have experimented with alternative forms of workplace governance. Joint health and safety committees are probably the most widespread example. There is also growing interest in using neutral facilitators to work with labour and management to discuss issues, solve problems, and make planning decisions outside the collective bargaining context. Also, 'preventive-mediation' programs are being developed as an alternative to the traditional dispute-resolution procedures.

Another positive step is the formation of institutions such as the Canadian Labour Market and Productivity Centre, national and provincial training boards, and sectoral councils. The model underlying each of these organizations involves business and labour representatives jointly addressing issues of mutual concern, again outside the collective bargaining process.[9] Until now, the focus of these groups has been limited to training alone. But training cannot be viewed separately from other HRM practices. The real challenge is to encourage the diffusion of all aspects of high-performance workplace models. A broadening of their focus will enhance the impact of these new institutions.

Incentives for Workplace Training

Training in the workplace is key for several reasons. First, it creates positive economic returns by developing human resources. Second, as the experiences of the new joint institutions described above have shown, there is a substantial overlap between the interests of management and labour in the area of training, which can provide a basis for building partnerships. And third, since training is highly correlated with other high-performance practices, it can lead to spillover effects by stimulating broader workplace change.

In Canada, governments have played a limited role in private-sector training. With concerns about public spending and possible windfalls for firms, this is probably as it should be. But there are some actions governments could take to increase employer-sponsored training, and in the process lever other high-performance HRM practices. These include:

- Continuing to back the training boards and sectoral councils would Raise the profile of training and encourage industry-based initiatives;
- Providing financial and coordinating support for small-employer training consortia, perhaps through the sectoral councils, could be an effective way to generate incremental training in a sector of the economy where current investment levels are low. By coordinating training plans and activities, small firms could overcome two major obstacles – the high cost of training and the scarcity of trainers, courses, and facilities;

- Targeting grants or tax credits should be considered, especially for small employers. The current tax incentive whereby expenditure on training is fully deductible offers no advantage to firms with no taxable income;[10] and
- Streamlining the program requirements and coordinating the programs offered by different levels of government.

Encourage Internal Responses to Shifting Business Conditions

Whereas firms in countries such as Japan and certain parts of Europe more often use internal adjustment mechanisms to adjust to changing business conditions, Canadian firms typically rely on layoffs. While there are clearly disadvantages to restricting employers' freedom to lay off workers,[11] Canada's policies and programs actually provide incentives to do so, while doing little to encourage adjusting internally.

One possible policy response to this problem is to experience-rate unemployment insurance. Currently, employers' premiums are unrelated to their layoff history. Consequently, the firm bears none of the direct costs associated with layoffs. Faced with a decline in labour needs, then, an employer faces no financial disincentive to let employees go. Experience-rating would direct some of these costs to firms, thereby encouraging them to consider internal alternatives to laying off workers.[12]

Policy-makers could also consider encouraging the redistribution of the available work within the firm as an adjustment mechanism. Paid educational leave and work-sharing, for example, are options that are compatible with the principles of the high-performance workplace model. Educational leave programs (jointly funded by the employee and the employer) contribute to human resource development, and if employees were encouraged to take such leave during downturns, they could also be an effective adjustment mechanism.

There is a federal work-sharing program already in place, which allows employers to reduce the hours of a group of employees who were to be laid off. They are paid UI benefits to partially compensate them for the reduction in wages. A recent evaluation of this program found that it has resulted in reduced layoffs. The evaluation found some problems with the program and recommended that it would be improved if the employees participating were more carefully targeted and more retraining was available to them (Ekos Research Associates 1993c).[13]

Strengthen Technical Education

High-performance workplace models are predicated on the existence of employees with good basic skills and the ability to learn. Workers who do not meet these standards will be passed up by the best employers and for the 'good jobs.' Moreover, as technological change increases the skills required, it will become even more important that there be an adequate educational base. Moreover, what constitutes an 'adequate' educational base is likely to change. The conventional notion of a 'dropout' as someone who has not completed high school may well have to be revised to include young people without at least some postsecondary education or vocational training. This makes it more urgent that we strengthen technical education and training as alternatives to university education.

Moving Forward on Family-Care Policies

Improving family-care benefits is essential to increase workers' productivity and reduce their levels of stress. The lack of affordable daycare and elder care is the most visible example of the problems workers experience trying to reconcile family and work responsibilities. While these issues (particularly daycare) have inspired a great deal of public debate, there has been little action. In the absence of adequate public resources, increasing demands are being placed on communities, families, and individuals.

Our research has shown that family-care benefits and flexible scheduling are rare among Canadian workplaces. This is particularly true of smaller organizations, where employers face genuine problems in providing flexibility and benefits. Public-policy makers will have to confront these shortcomings where the market does not offer a complete solution. The key elements include shorter working-time, access to benefits for nonstandard workers, and progress on expanding the quantity and quality of daycare.

Adopting High-Performance Systems within Government

Historically, governments as employers have often been models for the adoption of progressive labour practices. As such, they can play an important part in diffusing the high-performance workplace model. In some areas, such as providing family-care benefits and flexible scheduling, governments are already leaders. In others, such as encouraging employee involvement in decision-making and flexibility in work rules and job design, the traditional approaches still prevail. So governments, too, have a great deal to learn about human resource management.

Social Change: A Question of Will

Ultimately, our cultural and legal traditions limit the degree to which policy-makers can directly influence the diffusion of the high-performance workplace model. Workplace reform will simply not occur unless employers, workers, and unions are prepared to rethink and reshape longstanding roles, relationships, and responsibilities. This will involve tradeoffs for everyone, but ultimately the traditional arrangements are not compatible with the new economic, technological, and social realities.

Social change is not easy. It involves taking risks and changing attitudes, and poses far greater demands than other forms of innovation such as introducing new hardware. In part, this is why industry has not adopted genuine workplace reform to any great extent in its strategic response to the changing environment. If industry is to meet the new challenges successfully, however, this must change.

The issues we have examined in this study are also being debated in the US, Japan, and Europe. To varying degrees, all the advanced industrial nations now face the realization that workplace practices are at a crossroads. Choosing the correct path will involve major social reform in the workplace in order to catch up with the new economic and technological reality.

Notes

[1] For a review of employment security, see Buechtemann (1993).

[2] For a review of the evaluations of training programs in Canada and elsewhere, see OECD (1993).

[3] This is only one of the stresses facing Canadian families. For a comprehensive review, see Maxwell (1993).

[4] This is an extended version of the model developed by Verma and Weiler (1994) for the Human Resource Management Project.

[5] Marshall (1992) cites three reasons for this (1) workers are unlikely to go 'all out' unless they are confident of being protected from adverse conse-

quences; (2) cooperative, participative relationships cannot really exist between unequal partners; and (3) adversarial relations between workers and managers are inevitable and also functional where the interests of workers are represented.

[6] The most important bias in the HRPS sample is the underrepresentation of small firms, which, as our analysis shows, tend not to have high-performance workplace models. Further calculations that take this bias into account suggest that the real incidence of these two variants is closer to 30 percent.

[7] For a Canadian perspective on this 'new growth theory,' see Lipsey (1993).

[8] In discussing the disincentives arising from collective bargaining laws, O'Grady (1992) highlights the restrictions on the duty to bargain and the limitations of the union representation system.

[9] There are some differences among these organizations as to how business and labour are represented, the representation of other groups, and whether their role is purely advisory or extends to implementing action.

[10] Note that Quebec introduced a refundable tax credit for training in 1991. The credit can be applied to the cost of developing a training plan and formal training expenses. The level of the credit is higher for small- and medium-sized firms than for larger ones.

[11] Strong laws, for example, are often cited as an important reason for the stagnant employment growth in Europe compared with that in North America. There is little evidence that imposing such restrictions will lead to longer employee tenure (OECD 1993).

[12] An effective design for experience-rating would involve a number of considerations, but it would have to include fair arrangements for employers in seasonal industries.

[13] The major weakness identified in the evaluation was the tendency of some firms to use work-sharing programs to preserve the status quo, thereby avoiding restructuring.

Appendix A
Research Papers Prepared for the HRM Project

Gordon Betcherman and Gary J. Mac Donald, Queen's University. *HRM Trends in the Electrical and Electronic Products Sector: Results of the Human Resource Practices Survey*. HRM Project Series. Kingston, ON: IRC Press, Industrial Relations Centre, Queen's University, 1993.

Gordon Betcherman and Gary J. Mac Donald, Queen's University. *HRM Trends in the Wood Products Sector: Results of the Human Resource Practices Survey*. HRM Project Series. Kingston, ON: IRC Press, Industrial Relations Centre, Queen's University, 1993.

Gordon Betcherman, Kathryn McMullen and Norm Leckie, Queen's University. Out of Sync: Technological and Organizational Change in Canadian Industry. Queen's Papers in Industrial Relations, no. 1994-4. Kingston, ON: Industrial Relations Centre, Queen's University, 1994.

Gordon Betcherman, Norm Leckie, Queen's University, Anil Verma, University of Toronto. HRM Innovations in Canada: Evidence from Establishment Surveys. Queen's Papers in Industrial Relations, no. 1994-3. Kingston, ON: Industrial Relations Centre, Queen's University, 1994.

Christina Caron, Queen's University. Technological Change and Internal Labour Markets, 1980-1991. Unpublished background paper, 1993.

Rick Chaykowski and Brian Lewis, Queen's University. Canadian and US. Trends in Human Resource Management: Training and Compensation Practices. Unpublished background paper, 1994.

Bryan Downie and Mary Lou Coates, Queen's University. *Traditional and New Approaches to Human Resources Management*. HRM Project Series. Kingston, ON: IRC Press, Industrial Relations Centre, Queen's University, 1994.

Linda Duxbury, Carleton University and Christopher Higgins, University of Western Ontario. Part-Time Work for Women: Its Effects and Effectiveness. Unpublished background paper, 1994.

Ekos Research Associates Inc. Ontario Workplace Reorganization Survey. Unpublished background paper, 1993.

Ekos Research Associates Inc. Review of Federal and Provincial Programs Encouraging Employer-Sponsored Training in the Private Sector. Unpublished background paper, 1991.

Pradeep Kumar, Queen's University. *Unions and workplace change in Canada*. HRM Project Series. Kingston, ON: IRC Press, Industrial Relations Centre, Queen's University, 1994.

Marie Lavoie, École Polytechnique de Montréal. Impact of Internal Labour Market Arrangements on Technical Professionals' Performance in a Period of Transition. Unpublished background paper, 1993.

Norm Leckie, Queen's University. *The Choice of Human Resource Practices: Patterns, Determinants, and Outcomes*. HRM Project Series. Kingston, ON: IRC Press, Industrial Relations Centre, Queen's University, 1994.

An International Review of Labour Adjustment Policies and Practices. Queen's Papers in Industrial Relations, no. 1993-15. Kingston, ON: Industrial Relations Centre, Queen's University, 1993.

Norm Leckie and Gordon Betcherman, Queen's University. Impacts of HRM on Establishment Performance. Unpublished background paper, 1994.

Kathryn McMullen and Gary J. Mac Donald, Queen's University. *HRM Trends in the Business Services Sector: Results of the Human Resource Practices Survey*. HRM Project Series. Kingston, ON: IRC Press, Industrial Relations Centre, Queen's University, 1993.

Kathryn McMullen and Gary J. Mac Donald, Queen's University. *HRM Trends in the Fabricated Metal Products Sector: Results of the Human Resource Practices Survey*. HRM Project Series. Kingston,

ON: IRC Press, Industrial Relations Centre, Queen's University, 1993.

Kathryn McMullen, Norm Leckie and Christina Caron, Queen's University. *Innovation at Work: The Working with Technology Survey, 1980-91*. HRM Project Series. Kingston, ON: IRC Press, Industrial Relations Centre, Queen's University, 1993.

Linda Moffat, consultant. Competitive Strategy and Human Resources: A Review of the Management Literature. Unpublished background paper, 1991.

John O'Grady, consultant. *Job Control Unionism vs the New Human Resource Management Model: The Impact of Industrial Relations Factors on Changes in Work Organization in Manufacturing and Related Industries*. HRM Project Series. Kingston, ON: IRC Press, Industrial Relations Centre, Queen's University, 1994.

Ram Sharma, Queen's University. The Relationship Between Firm Size and HRM Practices, with Particular Attention on the Small-Firm Sector. Unpublished background paper, 1994.

Anil Verma, University of Toronto and Joseph Weiler, University of British Columbia. *Understanding Change in Canadian Industrial Relations: Firm-level Choices and Responses*. HRM Project Series. Kingston, ON: IRC Press, Industrial Relations Centre, Queen's University, 1994.

Terry Wagar, St. Mary's University. *Human Resource Management Practices and Organizational Performance: Evidence from Atlantic Canada*. HRM Project Series. Kingston, ON: IRC Press, Industrial Relations Centre, Queen's University, 1994.

Caroline Weber, Queen's University. *Effects of Personnel and Human Resource Management Practices on Firm Performance: A Review of the Literature*. HRM Project Series. Kingston, ON: IRC Press, Industrial Relations Centre, Queen's University, 1994.

Appendix B

Surveys Developed for the Human Resource Management Project

Three surveys were developed in-house for the HRM Project – the Human Resource Practices Survey (HRPS), the Working With Technology Survey (WWTS), and the Workplace Reorganization Survey (WRS). Descriptions of these surveys follow; technical details are summarized in Table B1.

The Human Resource Practices Survey

The HRPS is an establishment-level survey. It was conducted from February to April, 1993 by Canadian Facts.

The HRPS sample frame was based on the current Dun and Bradstreet list of Canadian establishments. The national sample included establishments with more than 40 employees. Four sectors were represented to reflect the range of industries in the Canadian economy.[1] The sectors surveyed were a resource group (wood products), a traditional manufacturing industry (fabricated metal products), a high value-added manufacturing industry (electrical and electronic products), and a dynamic service group (selected business services). The surveys in the latter two sectors were endorsed by two industry associations – the Electrical and Electronic Manufacturers' Association of Canada and the Information Technology Association of Canada, respectively.

Table B1

Technical Details of HRM Project Datasets

	Human Resources Practices Survey	Working with Technology Survey	Work Reorganization Survey
Sample size	714 establishments	224 establishments	206 union locals
Period covered	January 1988 – January 1993	1980-85, 1986-91	April 1988 – April 1993
Percentage distribution by number of employees[1]	1-49: 23 50-99: 36 100-249: 31 250+: 10	1-49: 18 50-100: 35 101-500: 38 501+: 8	40-119: 39 120+ : 34
Percentage distribution by industry	Wood products: 25 Fabricated metal products: 27 Electrical/electronic products: 20 Business services: 23	Forestry & mining: 4 Manufacturing: 43 Traditional services: 13 Dynamic services: 28 Health/social services: 9	Mining: 6 Metal manufacturing: 41 Other manufacturing: 45 Services: 9

[1] For the Work Reorganization Survey, percentage distribution by number of union members not employees.

Following an initial contact by telephone, questionnaires were sent to 1669 businesses. Of these, 714 returned usable responses, giving a response rate of 42.7 percent.

The contact point for each establishment was the senior person responsible for human resources. The respondents were asked to provide information for the preceding five years (since 1988) on a wide range of human resource issues, such as the role of the HRM function, training, job design, employee participation programs, compensation and incentive pay, fringe and family benefits, and non-standard work arrangements. Data were also gathered on the organizations' environments and various aspects of their performance.

The HRPS underrepresents very small firms, which, as our analysis shows, tend to have quite different human-resource arrangements and practices than larger organizations.

The Working With Technology Survey

The unique feature of the WWTS is that it is a longitudinal survey that collected data from a sample of establishments first in 1985 and then again in 1991. Each time, respondents were asked to provide information for the previous five years (1980-85 and 1986-91). The surveys were designed and conducted by the Economic Council of Canada.[2] In both periods, respondents were asked about their experiences with computer-based technological change and the resulting human-resource impacts.

The original 1985 sample was drawn from Dun and Bradstreet's listing of Canadian establishments. The sample frame covered every province and all sectors except agriculture, construction, and government; establishments with fewer than 20 employees were excluded. For the 1985 survey, responses were received from 946 establishments. In 1991, 224 of these establishments responded.[3] On all observable dimensions – industry, region, size, and ownership – the composition of the respondents and non-respondents to the second survey was very similar to that of the first. When compared with Statistics Canada data for the total population of business establishments, the WWTS underrepresents small establishments and over-represents the manufacturing sector.

Data for both WWTS periods were collected in questionnaires mailed to the senior managers of establishments. Telephone follow-ups were conducted among selected respondents. Data were collected about the type and cost of computer-based technological change (in office and process applications); planning for technological change and obstacles to its introduction; internal labour market adjustments, including hiring and training in response to changes in skill requirements; workplace innovation; and collective bargaining related to technological change.

The Workplace Reorganization Survey

The WRS was undertaken in cooperation with the United Steelworkers of America (USWA). The field work was carried out by Ekos Research Associates.

The survey was conducted by telephone in spring 1993. The sample, provided by the USWA, consisted of 328 presidents of Ontario locals, who were sent a letter from the district director encouraging them to participate in the study. The first 200 names were selected for the survey, and the rest were used to replenish the sample if people on the original list could not be contacted. The final dataset contains information from 206 USWA locals, a response rate of 89 percent. The majority (86 percent) of respondents represented workplaces in the manufacturing sector.

The questionnaire addressed workplace reorganization and environmental changes experienced over the previous five years (1988-93) by the companies where the respondents were the bargaining agents. The respondents were asked about the extent of union involvement in the changes and the impact of the changes on the local and its members. Background and contextual data were collected about such areas as the industry, union coverage, the number of employees, and the general state of the labour-management relationship in the bargaining unit.

Notes

[1] The HRPS did not include two other major parts of the economy – the public and quasi-public sectors and the 'traditional' services. Examples of the latter include retail trade, accommodation and food, and personal services. Pretests were carried out in traditional services; however, there were the questionnaire. Therefore this part of the survey was dropped. Our developmental work suggested that traditional services were less advanced in terms of HRM practices than the sectors that were surveyed.

[2] The 1985 and 1991 panel results are summarized in Betcherman and McMullen (1986) and McMullen, Leckie, and Caron (1993), respectively. Both surveys were conducted by the Economic Council of Canada. When that institution was closed in 1992, the survey database was transferred to the Industrial Relations Centre at Queen's University.

[3] In a longitudinal survey where data collection points are a number of years apart, establishments can be 'lost' for a number of reasons: shutdowns, mergers with other establishments, unrecorded relocations, or decisions not to respond to the follow up questionnaire. In the follow-up, we definitively identified 222 of the original 946 establishments as being no longer in business at an identifiable location in Canada. this left 724. Using the 724 establishments as an (upper-bound) estimate of the potential number of respondents to the follow-up, then, the 224 establishments returning a useable questionnaire (i.e., completed and matchable with a 1985 respondent) represent a response rate of 30 percent.

Appendix C1

Summary of Regression Results on the Relationship between the Introduction of Computer-Based Technologies (CBT) and Employees' Skill Levels

	Dependent variable					
	Highly skilled employees as a percentage of total employees, 1991	Change in the proportion of highly skilled employees 1985-1991	Unskilled employees as a percentage of total employment, 1991	Change in the proportion of unskilled employees 1985-1991	Index of skill level[1]	Index of skill increase[2]
% working with CBT	0.004***	0.002**	-0.004***	-0.002	0.008***	0.004**
WWT91 - WWT853	-0.001	-0.001	0.001	0.000	-0.001	-0.001
Proportion of highly skilled employees, 1985		-0.537***				0.855***
Proportion of unskilled employees, 1985				-0.797***	-0.465**	
R-square	.59	.57	.29	.55	.45	.57
Number of observations	119	99	119	99	119	99

Source: Estimates by the authors, based on data from the Working with Technology Survey.

[1] Proportion of highly skilled employees less proportion of unskilled employees.
[2] Change in proportion of highly skilled employees in the workforce less change in proportion of unskilled employees in the workforce.
[3] Proportion of employees in establishments working with computer-based technologies in 1991 less the proportion in 1985.
* Significant at the .10 level.   ** Significant at the .05 level.   *** Significant at the .01 level.

Appendix C2

Business Strategy Factor Scores[1] by Selected Establishment Characteristics

Characteristic	Factor		
	Process	Cost	Product
	(Mean standardized score)		
Sector			
Wood products	-0.096	0.205	-0.193
Fabricated metal products	0.031	0.220	-0.148
Electrical and electronic products	0.068	0.109	0.429
Selected business services	0.008	-0.475	0.002
Number of employees			
1-49	-0.139	0.007	-0.104
50-99	-0.096	-0.077	-0.007
100-249	0.130	-0.006	0.045
250+	0.236	0.423	0.009
Union status			
Union present	0.140	0.279	-0.074
No union	-0.094	-0.175	0.060

Source: Estimates by the authors, based on data from the Human Resource Practices Survey.

[1] Factor loadings are described in the text. Each establishment receives a score for each factor, based on the elements of its business strategy. Scores have been standardized to a mean of 0.000 for the complete sample.

Appendix C3

Summary of Logistic Regression Results on Establishments' Choice of HRM Cluster.

	HRM cluster		
	Traditional	Compensation	Participation
Sector[2]			
Wood products	1.232***	-0.983***	-0.652**
Fabricated metal products	1.206***	-0.669**	-0.867***
Electrical and electronic products	0.292	-0.650**	0.136
Size (number of employees)[1]			
1-49	0.354	-0.470	-0.107
100-249	-0.692***	0.562**	0.366
250+	-1.859***	1.766***	0.097
Union present[2]	-0.433*	0.073	0.438*
Region[2]			
Atlantic	-0.582	1.290***	-1.053
Quebec	0.522**	-0.973***	0.046
Prairies	-0.220	0.325	-0.085
British Columbia	-0.256	0.478	-0.124
Number of environmental changes	-0.106*	0.121*	0.009
Business strategy			
'Process'	-0.608***	0.203*	0.622***
'Cost'	-0.034	-0.181	0.213*
'Product'	-0.076	-0.066	0.178
Prediction rate (%)			
79.0			
77.0			
72.0			
Number of observations	597	597	597

Source: Estimates by the authors, based on data from the Human Resource Practices Survey.

[1] Selected business services, 50-99 employees, nonunionized status, and Ontario are the reference groups.
[2] Variable values are factor scores for each strategy.
* Significant at the .01 level.
** Significant at the .05 level.
*** Significant at the .10 level.

Appendix C4

Summary of Logistic Regression Results on Labour Performance Trends, 1988-93

	Dependent variable			
	Quits	Layoffs	Accidents	Grievances
HRM cluster[1]				
Participation-based	0.43**	0.54**	0.48**	0.19
Compensation-based	0.38*	0.07	0.31	0.21
Sector[2]				
Wood products	0.31	0.98***	2.41***	1.45***
Fabricated metal products	-0.13	0.42	1.88***	0.88***
Electrical and electronic products	0.35	0.08	1.73***	1.42***
Size (number of employees)[2]				
1-49	0.51**	0.08	-0.17	-0.34
100-249	0.54***	0.40	0.18	0.19
250+	1.19***	-0.48	0.37	0.46
Region[2]				
Atlantic	-1.05**	0.21	-0.10	-0.28
Quebec	-1.34***	-0.52	-0.14	-0.16
Prairies	-0.69***	-0.25	0.05	-0.28
British Columbia	-1.15***	-0.30	-0.89***	-0.72**
Union present[2]	0.00	0.23	0.19	0.66***
Prediction rate (%)	70.0	64.0	71.0	72.0
Number of observations	623	625	609	540

Source: Estimates by the authors, based on data from the Human Resource Practices Survey.

[1] The traditional HRM model, selected business services, 50-99 employees, Ontario, and nonunionized status are the reference groups.
* Significant at the .01 level.
** Significant at the .05 level.
*** Significant at the .10 level.

Appendix C5

Summary of Logistic Regression Results on Efficiency and Financial Performance Trends, 1988-93

	Dependent variable						
	Labour productivity	Unit costs	Customer complaints	Quality	Sales	Market share	Profits
HRM cluster[1]							
Participation-based	0.13	0.81***	0.14	-0.56	0.12	0.18	0.05
Compensation-based	0.34	0.81**	0.25	-0.58	-0.45	0.12	-0.37
Sector[1]							
Wood products	-0.04	0.25	-0.01	0.17	-0.06	0.11	-0.72**
Fabricated metal	-0.94*	0.49	-0.44	-0.43	-0.67**	-0.14	-0.92***
Electrical and electronic products	0.05	0.20	0.13	0.68	-0.21	0.02	-0.69**
Size (number of employees)[1]							
1-49	0.39	-0.47	0.53	-0.95	-0.83***	-0.86**	-0.36
100-249	0.16	-0.13	-0.50	-1.15*	-0.04	-0.25	-0.00
250+	0.49	-0.44	0.30	na2	-0.18	0.10	0.28
Region[1]							
Atlantic	-0.79	0.15	-0.54	-2.38**	0.38	0.24	0.03
Quebec	-0.27	-0.22	0.25	0.57	0.07	0.62	0.50
Prairies	1.13	0.46	-0.17	0.23	-0.02	0.00	0.34
British Columbia	-0.07	-0.15	-0.01	0.32	1.06***	0.63	0.66*
Union present[1]	0.37	0.06	0.25	0.37	-0.80***	-0.50	-0.22
Increasing competition	0.49	-0.33	-0.20	-1.54*	-0.73**	-1.18***	-0.81***
New technology					0.09	0.40	-0.10
Prediction rate (%)	68.0	64.0	62.0	76.0	69.0	67.0	65.0
Number of observations	302	293	221	284	381	262	335

Source: Estimates by the authors, based on data from the Human Resource Practices Survey.

[1] The traditional HRM model, selected business services, 50–99 employees, Ontario, and nonunionized status are the reference groups.
[2] Not applicable: no establishments with 250 employees and more among nonmissing observations.
* Significant at the .10 level.   ** Significant at the .05 level.   *** Significant at the .01 level.

References

Arthur, J.B. 1992. The link between business strategy and industrial relations systems in American steel minimills. *Industrial and Labor Relations Review* 45:488-506.

Betcherman, G. 1993. Research gaps facing training policy-makers. *Canadian Public Policy* 1993: 18-28.

Betcherman, G. and G.J. Mac Donald. 1993a. *HRM trends in the wood sector: Results of the human resource practices survey.* HRM Project Series. Kingston, ON: IRC Press, Industrial Relations Centre, Queen's University.

Betcherman, G. and G.J. Mac Donald. 1993b. *HRM trends in the electrical and electronic products sector: Results of the human resource practices survey.* HRM Project Series. Kingston, ON: IRC Press, Industrial Relations Centre, Queen's University.

Betcherman, G., N. Leckie and A. Verma. 1994. HRM innovations in Canada: evidence from establishment surveys. Queen's Papers in Industrial Relations, no. 1994-3, Kingston, ON: Industrial Relations Centre, Queen's University.

Betcherman, G. and K. McMullen. 1986. *Working with technology: A survey of automation in Canada.* A Research Report prepared for the Economic Council of Canada. Ottawa: Supply and Services Canada.

Betcherman, G., K. McMullen and N. Leckie. 1994. Out of sync: Technological and organizational change in Canadian industry. Queen's Papers in Industrial Relations, no. 1994-4, Kingston, ON: Industrial Relations Centre, Queen's University.

Buechtemann, C.F., ed. 1993. *Employment security and labor market behavior: Interdisciplinary approaches and international evidence.* Ithaca, NY: ILR Press, Cornell University.

Canadian Labour Market and Productivity Centre. 1993. *National training survey.* Ottawa: CLMPC.

Caron, C. 1993. Technological change and internal labour markets, 1980-91. Unpublished background paper for the Human Resource Management Project, Ottawa.

Chaykowski, R.P. and A. Verma, eds. 1992. *Industrial relations in Canadian industry.* Toronto: Holt, Rinehart, and Winston Canada.

Chaykowski, R.P. and B. Lewis. 1994. Canadian and US trends in human resource management: training and compensation practices. Unpublished background paper for the Human Resource Management Project, Ottawa.

Cooke, W. 1990. *Labor-management cooperation.* Kalamazoo, MI: Upjohn Institute.

Downie, B. and M.L. Coates. 1994. *Traditional and new approaches to human resource management.* HRM Project Series. Kingston, ON: IRC Press, Industrial Relations Centre, Queen's University.

Dunlop, J.T. 1958. *Industrial relations systems.* New York: Holt, Rinehart, and Winston.

Duxbury, L. and C. Higgins. 1994. Part-time work for women: Its effects and effectiveness. Unpublished background paper for the Human Resource Management Project, Ottawa.

Eaton, A.E. and P.B. Voos. 1992. Unions and contemporary innovations in work organization, compensation, and employee participation. In *Unions and economic competitiveness*, edited by L. Mishel and P.B. Voos, pp.173-215. Armonk, NY: M.E. Sharpe.

Economic Council of Canada. 1991. *Employment in the service economy.* Ottawa: Supply and Services Canada.

Ekos Research Associates. 1993a. Reskilling society: Industrial perspectives. Unpublished report for the Public Affairs Branch, Employment and Immigration Canada.

Ekos Research Associates. 1993b. Ontario workplace reorganization survey. Unpublished background paper for the Human Resource Management Project, Ottawa.

Ekos Research Associates. 1993c. Work sharing evaluation. Unpublished report for the Program Evaluation Branch, Employment and Immigration Canada.

Gunderson, M. 1993. Efficient instruments for labour market regulation. Discussion Paper no.93-05, Government and Competitiveness Project, School of Policy Studies, Queen's University.

Higgins, C., L. Duxbury, and C. Lee. 1992. Balancing work and family: A study of Canadian private sector employees. Unpublished report for the National Centre for Management Research and Development, University of Western Ontario.

Kapsalis, C. 1993. Employee training in Canada: Reassessing the evidence. *Canadian Business Economics* (summer):3-11.

Kochan, T.A., H.C. Katz and R.B. McKersie. 1986. *The transformation of American industrial relations.* New York: Basic Books.

Kumar, Pradeep. 1993. *From uniformity to divergence: Industrial relations in Canada and the United States.* Kingston, ON: IRC Press, Industrial Relations Centre, Queen's University.

Kumar, P. 1994. *Unions and workplace change in Canada.* HRM Project Series. Kingston, ON: IRC Press, Industrial Relations Centre, Queen's University.

Ichniowski, C., K. Shaw and G. Prennushi. 1993. The effects of human resource management practices on productivity. Unpublished paper, Columbia University.

Leckie, N. 1993. An international review of labour adjustment policies and practices. Queen's Papers in Industrial Relations, no. 1993-15. Kingston, ON: Industrial Relations Centre, Queen's University.

Leckie, N. 1994. *The choice of human resource practices: patterns, determinants, and outcomes.* HRM Project Series. Kingston, ON: IRC Press, Industrial Relations Centre, Queen's University.

Leckie, N. and G. Betcherman. 1994. HRM practices and firm performance. Unpublished background paper for the Human Resource Management Project, Ottawa.

Lipsey, R.G. 1993. Globalization, technological change and economic growth. *Canadian Business Economics* (fall):3-17.

MacDuffie, J.P and J. Krafcik. 1992. Integrating technology and human resources for high-performance manufacturing. In *Transforming organizations,* edited by T. Kochan and M. Useem, pp.210-26. New York: Oxford University Press.

Macy, B.A., P.D. Bliese and J.J Norton. 1991. Organizational change and work innovation: A meta-analysis of 131 North American field experiments – 1961-1990. Paper presented at the National Academy of Management Meeting, Miami.

Marshall, R. 1992. Work organization, unions, and economic performance. In *Unions and economic competitiveness*, edited by L. Mishel and B. Voos, pp.287-315. Armonk, NY: M.E. Sharpe.

Maxwell, J. 1993. Globalization and family security. In National Forum on Family Security, *Family Security in Insecure Times*, pp.19-55. Ottawa: Canadian Council on Social Development.

McMullen, K. and G.J Mac Donald. 1993a. *HRM trends in the fabricated metal products sector: Results of the human resource practices survey.* HRM Project Series. Kingston, ON: IRC Press, Industrial Relations Centre, Queen's University.

McMullen, K. and G.J Mac Donald. 1993b. *HRM trends in the business services sector: Results of the human resource practices survey.* HRM Project Series. Kingston, ON: IRC Press, Industrial Relations Centre, Queen's University.

McMullen, K., N. Leckie and C. Caron. 1993. *Innovation at work: The with technology survey, 1980-91.* HRM Project Series. Kingston, ON: IRC Press, Industrial Relations Centre, Queen's University.

Mincer, J. 1988. *Job training, wage growth, and labor turnover.* Working Paper no.2690, National Bureau of Economic Research, Cambridge, MA.

Morissette, R., J. Myles and G. Picot. 1993. What is happening to earnings inequality in Canada? Research Paper No. 60, Business and Labour Market Analysis Group, Statistics Canada. Ottawa: Supply and Services Canada.

O'Grady, J. 1992. Economic restructuring and industrial relations in the province of Ontario: Removing the obstacles to negotiated adjustments. Unpublished report for International Institute for Labour Studies, Geneva.

O'Grady. J. 1994. *Job control unionism vs. the new human resource management model: The impact of industrial relations factors on changes in work organization in manufacturing and related industries.* HRM Project Series. Kingston, ON: IRC Press, Industrial Relations Centre, Queen's University.

OECD. 1991. *Employment outlook.* Paris: OECD.

OECD. 1993. *Employment outlook.* Paris: OECD.

Osterman, P. 1988. *Employment futures: Reorganization, dislocation, and public policy.* New York: Oxford University Press.

Porter, M. 1990. *The competitive advantage of nations*. New York: The Free Press.

Rechnitzer, E. 1990. *Human resource training and development survey results*. Catalogue No.81-574E, Statistics Canada. Ottawa: Supply and Services Canada.

Riddell, W.C. 1992. Unionization in Canada and the United States: A tale of two countries. Discussion Paper no.92-37, Department of Economics, University of British Columbia, Vancouver.

Troy, L. 1992. Convergence in industrial unionism etc: The case of Canada and the USA. *British Journal of Industrial Relations* 30:1-43.

US Department of Labor. 1993. *Report on high performance work practices and firm performance*. Washington: Bureau of National Affairs.

Verma, A and J.M. Weiler. 1994. *Understanding change in Canadian industrial relations: Firm-level choices and responses*. HRM Project Series. Kingston, ON: IRC Press, Industrial Relations Centre, Queen's University.

Wagar, T.H. 1994. *Human resource management practices and organizational performance: Evidence from Atlantic Canada*. HRM Project Series. Kingston, ON: IRC Press, Industrial Relations Centre, Queen's University.

Weber, C.L. 1994. *Effects of personnel and human resource management practices on firm performance: A review of the literature*. HRM Project Series. Kingston, ON: IRC Press, Industrial Relations Centre, Queen's University.